Cut & Thrust

Cut & Thrust

European Swords and Swordsmanship

Martin J. Dougherty

AMBERLEY

First published 2014

Amberley Publishing
The Hill, Stroud
Gloucestershire, GL5 4EP

www.amberley-books.com

Copyright © Martin J. Dougherty 2014

The right of Martin J. Dougherty to be identified as the Author
of this work has been asserted in accordance with the
Copyrights, Designs and Patents Act 1988.

All rights reserved. No part of this book may be reprinted
or reproduced or utilised in any form or by any electronic,
mechanical or other means, now known or hereafter invented,
including photocopying and recording, or in any information
storage or retrieval system, without the permission in writing
from the Publishers.

British Library Cataloguing in Publication Data.
A catalogue record for this book is available from the British Library.

ISBN 978 1 4456 3966 6 (print)
ISBN 978 1 4456 3978 9 (ebook)

Typeset in 11pt on 12pt Sabon.
Typesetting and Origination by Amberley Publishing.
Printed in the UK.

Contents

	Foreword	7
	Introduction	9
1	Swords and Swordsmanship	15
2	The Empire and the Arena: The Roman Gladius	37
3	Bright Blades in a Dark Age: The Warrior's Sword	51
4	Blades of Chivalry: The Medieval Longsword	75
5	The Art of Defence: Swords of the Renaissance	97
6	A Gentleman's Companion: The Small-Sword	123
7	Ye True Fyght: Cutting Swords	151
8	Alive and Well: Fencing in the Modern Era	177

Foreword

Any book on a subject so large and diverse as European swordsmanship must of necessity contain numerous generalisations, and can be at best an overview of the subject. Closer examination of any of the weapons or the periods of history discussed here will reveal wondrous new levels of complexity which, in turn, will be found to lead ever deeper into a truly fascinating subject.

Terminology, in particular, is a minefield for the modern scholar. Most of the labels we put on weapons are of modern origin; at the time they might simply have been referred to as 'swords', because everyone knew what was being described. A gentleman did not compare his 'late transition rapier' to that of a friend; they admired one another's swords, perhaps using terms now lost to us.

Any given term might be used imprecisely by those writing in the period, or its meaning might shift over time. This was not much of a problem for those living in the era; they would understand the context. But for us, looking back over the vast sweep of history, there is a need to create distinctions that perhaps did not exist when the weapons we are studying were in use. Let us not forget that the evolution of swords and swordsmanship was a constant process, rather than a series of neat jumps from one type to another, and terminology also drifted rather than being redefined and updated for the convenience of later scholars.

For a work of this sort, we must try to differentiate weapons one from another by using sensible labels, but we must not forget that within each type there was endless variation – one backsword was not necessarily exactly like another. We must deal in generalisations here, and allow the tantalising glimpse of deeper truths and greater complexity to lead us into further study.

This work is aimed at anyone with an interest in the reality of European swordsmanship: the historian, the re-enactor or the fencer; the reader or writer of 'sword-related fiction'. It was compiled partly through historical research and partly through hands-on training. For the latter, much is owed to the instructors and members of the British Federation of Historical Swordplay, notably:

Bob Brooks
Phil Crawley
Ian Macintyre
Greig Watson
My colleagues at the Durham chapter of the Society for the Study of Swordsmanship

Thanks are also owed to Steve Thurston, Michael Whittaker and Gavin Lanata for making the images happen.

And of course there are the many students, opponents and instructors I have encountered in over twenty-five years of what I like to call 'swording'. These are the people I learned from, at times experimented upon, and far too frequently met spectacular defeat at the hands of. Hopefully I learned something along the way…

Martin J. Dougherty, September 2014.

Introduction

Of all the weapons ever invented, none has the mystique of the sword. It remains a symbol of authority and strength long after its day on the battlefield has passed. Swords feature in figures of speech, in statues and monuments, and in company logos. They are used in solemn ceremonies and hung on walls as decorations. The sword remains a potent symbol of authority, strength and power.

Yet the word 'sword' can actually mean entirely different things to different people. The Japanese katana, the Roman gladius and the Scottish claymore are all swords, and they are all quite different from one another. The khopesh of ancient times, though quite likely the first weapon known as a 'sword', does not resemble any of the weapons a modern person would recognise as one. It could be argued that many of the implements known as swords are so different from one another, and are used so differently, that they constitute an entirely separate group of weapons.

There are, however, some similarities. Swords are weapons intended to cut or puncture the target, and rely on concentration of force at a sharp edge or point to do so. They have a metal blade, which can be curved or straight, and usually feature some form of protection for the user's hand. This also defines knives, which is not surprising since the basic form of the sword, consisting of a handle and a blade, is essentially that of an overgrown knife.

Matters are further complicated by the fact that some knives are large enough to be considered sword-type weapons, and there is some debate about exactly how much blade is necessary before a knife becomes a sword. Some weapons, such as machetes, are highly similar to swords but are not described as such, and are usually considered to be a distinct and separate weapon type.

As a useful working definition, a blade weapon becomes a sword when it satisfies enough (or perhaps even all) of these criteria:

It has a metal blade running the length of the weapon, and a handgrip.
The blade is a single piece, i.e. there is no haft and head in the manner of an axe.
It has enough blade length to extend the user's reach significantly on a thrust or cut.
It has enough mass to make a cut bite into the target.
It has enough mass to be used to parry an attack, and is large enough to reliably stop one.
It has significant protection for the user's hand.
It is too large to be carried concealed.

This is not a hard-and-fast definition, but such a thing is always going to be elusive when even apparently specific terms like 'rapier' or 'sabre' can actually refer to a range of somewhat dissimilar weapons. Perhaps all that can be said with certainty is that a sword is a metal-bladed cutting or thrusting implement large enough to be considered a combat weapon, rather than an emergency expedient or a tool that could be pressed into service at need.

Not all swords fulfil all the criteria noted above. Many have no point, no edge, or virtually no hand protection. Some Eastern and Asian weapons are highly exotic and push the boundaries of what can rightly be considered a sword. For this reason we will consider only European swords – although those have, at times, been the subject of external influences – and we will begin our examination of swords and swordsmanship at a time when the sword had taken on at least one of its modern forms.

There have been various attempts to impose a rational terminology on sword types, although this presents an enormous challenge for various reasons. Idiom and the difficulty of translating from one language to another have created bastardised terms or corrupted names, while some apparently descriptive terms actually mean different things at different times. For example, it seems reasonable to describe the gladius hispaniensis of the Roman soldier as a 'short sword', but the term was also applied at times to the knightly arming sword, which was a full-length combat sword whose blade might be 50 per cent longer than the gladius. The arming sword was 'short' in comparison with the two-handed longsword, so the distinction made sense in its context, but it causes confusion to those looking back over all of history.

Terms like broadsword seem like a logical distinction, so it might be assumed that the term was used at the time during which the weapon it describes was in service. However, this is not always so. The term broadsword was imposed by relatively recent historians to describe various broad-bladed cutting swords, but was probably not used by the people who fought with those weapons.

The most notable attempt to map the riddle-maze that is sword terminology was put forward by Ewart Oakeshott in 1960. The Oakeshott Typology categorised the swords of the Middle Ages into thirteen distinct types, using their physical characteristics as a guide. This system was combined with the work of earlier historians who did the same for 'Viking' swords to create a system that places weapons in distinct groups, labelled I to XXII.

However, while the Oakeshott Typology may be of enormous value to museum staff and historical researchers, Roman numerals are not very descriptive and may not suit the layman. A work of fiction describing the battles of a noble knight armed with his faithful Oakeshott Type XX might someday be written, but for most purposes a more general terminology will serve quite well.

Thus, we will use modern descriptive terms such as longsword, broadsword and the like, knowing that these are in many cases not what the weapon was called in its day. While terminology of this sort is a little loose, if used logically based on the weapon's physical characteristics it will indicate the general appearance and mode of use of the weapon. For creators of games, movies and fiction, and for most historical fencers, re-enactors and the like, this general terminology is entirely sufficient.

It is worth remembering that terminology did vary by time and place, and that once close examination is made of any weapon or era it may be necessary to consider subtypes, variants and exceptions to the general rule. Contemporary terms are useful in describing specific weapons, but when considering the evolution of the sword, a more general approach is necessary.

The key factor that allowed the modern long-bladed sword to develop was of course metallurgy. A knife blade, spear point or axe head can be made from a relatively small or very solid piece of metal, and is thus unlikely to break under the stresses of combat. As blade length increases, so does the difficulty of creating a weapon that will remain useful after a couple of blows.

To be effective, a sword blade must be able to take a good sharp point and/or edge, and to keep it despite contact with flesh, shields, armour, opposing weapons or anything else that may be struck – deliberately or otherwise. If the blade is too soft it will simply flex and remain bent; too hard and it will crack or even shatter.

The very first 'swords' actually resembled a hand axe in many ways. The blade was of a single piece of metal, however, and was bellied forward to create a striking surface. This weapon, known as a sickle-sword, khopesh or sapphara, was initially made of bronze, though some later examples did use iron. The sickle-sword was used to make slashing cuts rather than hacking like an axe, and might well have bent on overzealous contact.

It is 'swords' of this type that are referred to in ancient texts such as the Old Testament of the Bible or the records of Ancient Egypt. Later eras have reimagined the people of these times fighting with more modern cruciform swords, leading to many depictions that are in fact quite wrong. However, the method of use was more sword than axe, and these weapons required skilled craftsmanship to make. They were the top-end military weapon systems of the day, and as such were status symbols as much as they were tools for combat.

Improvements in metalworking, and increased understanding of how to work iron, allowed the humble knife to grow into a more effective replacement for the sickle-sword. As blade lengths increased, the weapon had to either be able to flex and return to its normal shape unharmed, or be heavily constructed and fairly short.

In time, weapons like the Iberian falcata or the Greek kopis appeared. These had a forward curve on the blade, which was not of uniform width. This construction method concentrated the force of a blow near the tip of the weapon, but also allowed the blade to slide and cut. The overall form of the Greek kopis is not enormously different to that of the khopesh, or sickle-sword, but there is an obvious evolution towards the modern form of the sword. Some machetes and similar weapons still use this blade form, and it remains very effective.

However, by the time that the Roman Republic had become an empire, its troops (as well as many of its enemies) were armed with a true sword. The Roman sword was short by modern standards, and lacked much in the way of hand protection, but the gladius was extremely effective in combat. So effective, in fact, that its users could often outfight swordsmen equipped with longer weapons. The advantage may not have been so much in the design of the weapon as in how it was used … but then those two factors are always intertwined.

As we shall see in the coming chapters, there are as many approaches to swordsmanship as there are designs of sword. What they all have in common is the means by which a sword causes damage to the target, and the basic principles that underlie every successful sword-fighting system.

CHAPTER 1
Swords and Swordsmanship

There are many possible weapons that can be put in the hand of a warrior. Some are better suited to certain tasks than others, yet all of them are designed to do the same thing – to incapacitate or kill an opponent. The two are, to a great extent, linked, and it requires a high level of weapons technology to create a 'less lethal' weapon that will reliably put down its target without being likely to also cause permanent injury.

In truth, until the creation of modern weapon systems there were no really effective 'less lethal' weapons. Not killing an opponent required more skill than giving him a disabling wound that he might or might not die from, or else intimidating him into surrender by creating a situation where he could see he was defeated.

In an environment where armed combat was a life-or-death matter, lethality was actually not always the foremost concern of the weapon designer. What was critically important was the ability to incapacitate an opponent without being hit by a return blow. Death was a secondary concern; what mattered was putting the opponent out of the fight. If he fell to the ground and stayed there for the duration of a battle, that was a better result than an opponent who struck a few more blows and then fell.

The lethality of the sword as a weapon, and its unsuitability to 'less lethal' situations, is mainly due to the mechanisms by which weapons cause harm. There are four broadly defined mechanisms; three of them cause the target's skin to be broken by a sharp blade or point. This will, at the very least, cause bleeding and the risk of infection, and may cause trauma to muscles and other tissues that will never properly heal without surgery – assuming of course that the target is not killed by his injuries.

The fourth mechanism, blunt force, can sometimes be used to inflict a knockout blow by striking the head. However, a slight misjudgement can result in the blow either failing to do more than annoy the target, or causing a skull fracture and probably death. Blows to other parts of the body, such as the legs or shoulder area, with a blunt implement like a baton or the flat of a sword can subdue the target through pain and muscle trauma. However, this can take several blows and still risks inflicting an unintentional but nevertheless serious injury.

The mechanisms by which weapons cause harm can be loosely defined as:

Impaling
Slashing
Hacking
Impact

These mechanisms are defined by the concepts of force, impact and pressure, all of which are interrelated. The weight of a moving weapon, and how fast it is travelling, defines the amount of kinetic energy it has. When it strikes home, this energy is transferred to the target and may cause tissues, bone and the like to deform.

A very heavy object moving slowly and a very light one moving fast can have the same amount of kinetic energy, but the large one will tend to push the target (which could possibly crush it against something), whereas the faster object tends to transfer its energy more quickly and creates an impact.

The faster a weapon dumps its energy into the target, the more damage is done. This is largely because a slow, 'pushy' impact will move the target away from the blow or allow nearby flesh to deform in an elastic manner. Flesh and body tissues can dissipate a fair amount of energy without coming to much harm if allowed to do so over a period of time. The same amount of energy delivered as an almost instantaneous impact will cause severe trauma.

This of course assumes a perfectly blunt instrument, and in practice few weapons are entirely without projections. Even a mace, perhaps the archetypical blunt-force weapon, may have spikes or flanges to concentrate force, and thus will harm the target by a combination of blunt and sharp force.

When force is concentrated at a sharp point, the amount of pressure exerted is greatly increased. This is why it is possible to push a drawing pin into a wall with your thumb, provided it is the right way round. An amount of force that can drive a pin into the wall would penetrate flesh easily, but if it is spread out over a large area then it cannot do so.

A point or edge on a weapon concentrates force in this manner. The moving mass of the weapon defines how much force it can deliver, and the sharpness of the point or edge translates that into pressure at a given spot. Pressure allows the weapon to punch deep into flesh with relative ease, seeking internal organs that can be punctured. The torso is especially vulnerable to such stabbing wounds; a penetration of just 5 cm can find a vital organ or artery, and 15 cm of penetration is likely to, especially in the chest cavity.

Of course, a very sharp point does not rely on kinetic energy at all. A blunt weapon that is placed against the skin and pushed will not achieve anything useful, but a sharp point may slide into flesh with very little force behind it. Thus injuries can be considered to follow a continuum from perfect blunt force to perfect sharp force, with the blunt end requiring a certain amount of weapon mass and the sharp end requiring virtually none.

What, then, of the edge? The edge of a weapon can be considered much like an infinite series of sharp points, and can cause injury in two primary ways. If the weapon is swung hard, much like a blunt instrument, then the effects of its impact will be magnified by the sharp edge, which concentrates the force of the weapon into extreme pressure along the line of impact. A 'hacking' (also termed 'shearing' or 'percussive') blow of this sort will bite deep into flesh, benefiting from both the heavy impact and the sharp edge.

A lighter blade, lacking the mass to deliver a powerful blow, will not penetrate very deeply if used in this manner. It will rapidly be brought to a stop by the resilience of the target's flesh. In order to cause serious injury, the weapon must move in contact with flesh, using a slicing motion to cause the blade to cut. A longer blade allows a deeper cut, as the blade slices the whole time it is moving in contact with the target. 'Slashing' blows of this type are delivered with the intent of making the blade slide across flesh rather than smashing into it.

Most edged weapons use a combination of slashing and hacking. An axe can be considered a pure hacking weapon, more or less, as its design is totally focused on delivering maximum force behind a sharp edge, punching the blade into flesh rather than slicing it open. A sharp axe blade can be used to slash, but this is a waste of the weapon's potential.

Swords, on the other hand, tend to be able to both hack and slash, sometimes in the same blow. An unskilled user will tend to deliver a hacking blow no matter what the weapon is designed for, and this may not be all that effective. A more skilled swordsman learns to push or draw a cut, using the impact of the weapon to bite into flesh and then drawing as much blade as possible through the wound to deepen and lengthen it.

As a general rule, the sharper a weapon is, the less kinetic energy it needs to cause damage, i.e. a very sharp point or edge can kill or disable an opponent with little effort, whereas a blunt weapon requires either more mass or more force, or both. It is not a coincidence that the sword-making art has produced weapons capable of taking and holding a sharp edge or point rather than nicely shaped but blunt metal clubs.

However, weapon designers also had to consider a number of other factors, not least of which was the ability of the user to carry and effectively wield a weapon. Most swords are carried as sidearms rather than as the main combat weapon. That is to say, if the user were expecting to fight a battle then he would probably equip himself with a 'battlefield' weapon. Depending on the era this might be an axe or spear, a large mace or lance, an arquebus, or even a rifle. He would fall back on his sword only if necessary.

Some swords are large and potent enough to be considered 'battlefield' weapons, i.e. they have the reach and the capability to cause injury through the armour of the day and are thus highly effective in open combat. However, many of these swords are also too large to be carried as a sidearm. They would be taken into battle or a threatening situation, but when the owner was about his daily business he would probably carry something less clumsy.

Thus, swords need to strike a balance between ease of carrying and effectiveness as a combat weapon. There is a limit to how long a weapon can be and still be drawn quickly at need. Another consideration is where the weapon may have to be used. An open battlefield usually has plenty of room to whirl a flail or swing a two-handed axe, but the alleys of a town are a different matter.

There is also the question of usability. A sword is a large, heavy piece of metal, and is tiring to use even for a swordsman who is well conditioned by constant practice. A tired sword arm results in weak, ineffective blows or inaccurate ones. It causes thrusts to miss due to mistakes or because the opponent saw the clumsy attack coming and evaded. It makes parries late or weak, and can thus open up the swordsman for a killing strike.

A sword, then, cannot be too heavy if it is to remain effective after a couple of exchanges. As a rule, fights are won by the swordsman who keeps good control of his weapon for longest. A well-controlled sword can slip through a small opening and land a telling blow, whereas a wild swing might be extremely dangerous for anyone nearby but can often be parried or avoided with minimal effort.

A long blade gives good reach, allowing the opponent to be hit from a safe distance, and a heavy blade delivers a lot of impact that can push aside an opponent's weapon and deliver a powerful blow. However, length comes at the cost of weight, and weight makes a sword slower and more tiring to use. Length of blade can be translated into time to react, but a heavy sword cannot change direction as quickly as a light one and cannot take advantage of opportunities in the way that a lighter weapon can.

Thus there are many factors that can give one sword an advantage over another. Speed, reach, powerful impact and ease of use are a few, along with what might be described as 'handiness' at close quarters. Different weapons are suited to different applications, and one sword is not necessarily better than another. Ultimately, the swordsman who makes best use of the advantages his weapon gives him will emerge victorious.

Components of the Sword

A sword, in the simplest terms, consists of a blade and a hilt. There are many sub-components of course, and not every weapon has all of them. Names for the various parts of the weapon have also varied from country to country over time. Some components (or words for them) are unique to a particular weapon, era or place. What follows is thus a general overview of the main parts of the weapon.

The blade is composed of a single piece, though during the forging process a blade may be constructed from separate parts. For example, Norse swordsmiths would place strips of very hard steel down the edges of a softer blade, creating an area that would take and hold an edge. A blade made wholly of such steel would be difficult to make and would probably not be flexible enough to survive combat.

Part of the blade, known as the tang, is designed to fit inside the handgrip and hold the parts of the weapon together. If the tang is too weak or too small there is a real risk that the sword will bend or simply snap off just in front of the hilt when it encounters a solid parry or makes one. Although hidden, the tang is a vitally important part of the blade.

The blade itself may or may not have a sharp point. Most swords have some kind of point, though it may be quite rounded and not well suited to thrusting. It is thus fairly obvious whether or not a sword is intended for thrusting – a straight blade and a good point are strong indications, though by no means all straight swords are meant for this purpose. All the same, even a rounded point can punch into flesh if the user tries hard enough, and if an opportunity presents itself, most blades can deliver a reasonable thrust.

The main part of the blade is normally considered to consist of three principal sections, though some sword-fighting styles do not much care about the distinction. The part nearest the handgrip is often known as the 'forte' or 'strong', which describes it very well. Not only is the blade itself strongest near the hilt, but this is the part of the blade best suited to apply force to an opponent's blade or resist it. Parries are usually executed with the forte.

The middle of the blade is not named in many systems, but is referred to as 'mezzo' or 'middle' in some. In reality, some parries fall on this area of the blade, which is not much of a problem unless trying to stop a heavy blow with a lighter sword. The further towards the point that force is applied, the greater leverage the opponent has, which may result in the weapon being moved aside, so the mezzo is not the ideal place to receive a cut.

Blows in the mezzo area of a weapon are most likely to bend or break it, as the blade will flex along its length. A blow with a heavy weapon near the tip will push the blade to the side rather than making it flex, and the forte is, as already noted, the strongest part of the weapon. The area near the tip is known as the 'foible' or 'feeble' in many fencing styles. It is the weakest part of the blade and cannot be used to parry effectively under most circumstances.

On swords designed for cutting, there is an area, typically about two-thirds to three-quarters of the way to the tip, known as the 'point of percussion'. This is where the mezzo and the foible meet and is the point at which a cut is most effective, due to the shape and construction of the blade. The force of a cut is most focused at this point, and the blade will slide and cut more effectively. The exact location of the point of percussion depends on the shape and construction of the blade, the weight of the hilt, and the general balance of the weapon as a whole.

Cutting and hacking swords may be referred to as double-edged or single-edged, depending on whether they have two or one main cutting edges. The main cutting surface is known as the 'true edge' or 'long edge' and faces in the direction of a natural swing with the weapon, i.e. away from the user if the weapon is held in the hand pointing straight upwards. The other edge, known as the 'false edge' or 'short edge', is not sharpened in some weapons, or only sharpened for a short distance to allow opportunistic cuts with the tip of the weapon.

Even if a sword has no edges at all and is purely intended for thrusting, the concept of the 'true' and 'false' edges remains important to swordsmanship. The true edge is normally used to parry, as this places both the sword and the user's hand in their strongest orientation relative to an incoming cut. Some parries are made with the false edge, notably against thrusts where there is no danger of a weak hand position resulting in a dropped sword.

Parrying with the edge does result in a weapon becoming nicked and blunted, and maintenance is required if the weapon is not to become ineffective or break. However, true-edge parries are highly effective in stopping incoming cuts and are far less likely to result in a lost or even snapped sword than when placing the weapon side-on to an attack.

As already noted, at the user's end of the blade is the tang, which fits inside the handgrip. The grip itself can vary considerably and may be highly decorative. Grips are often wrapped with leather or wire. Behind the grip, there is usually some kind of pommel. This may be a simple ball or disc, but may be a decorative item; either way it acts as a counterweight to the blade. It can also be used to strike, and very occasionally it catches a cut that might otherwise have slid under a parry. This is usually a matter of good fortune; deliberately parrying with the pommel seems a little too chancy.

Between the grip and the blade there is usually some kind of hand protection. This varies from a small disc or crosspiece to an elaborate and sometimes fanciful arrangement of metal bars and wires. As a general rule, in periods where the common mode of swordsmanship is cutting, or swords are used in conjunction with a shield, then swords tend to have simple or even no hand protection. Where the sword is commonly used for both attack and defence, and thrusts are likely, greater hand protection is common to prevent a blade sliding up the weapon and slicing the user's fingers off. The hilt also helps protect the rest of the user when the weapon is pushed forward on a thrust, by blocking off some avenues of attack.

The most basic form of hand protection is a disc or some kind of crosspiece, which may well be very small. This is sufficient in most cases to prevent a blade sliding up to the hand, though many sword designs have quite long projections, known as quillions. Many styles of swordsmanship require that one or two fingers are actually in front of the quillions, resting on a blunt part of the blade known as a ricasso. Additional hand protection ahead of the ricasso then becomes necessary.

Quillions can be used to bind an opponent's blade by locking it between the blade and the crosspiece, controlling it while a counter-attack is made. They can also be used to strike, using a punching motion, and some styles of swordsmanship make use of the crosspiece to hook or trip the opponent. This requires holding the weapon by the blade, and is commonest with blunt-bladed swords or where users wear armoured gauntlets.

Additional hand protection may be provided by a knuckle bow, which can be a simple stirrup-shaped loop of metal or may be quite elaborate. The knuckle bow prevents an opponent's blade from striking the user's hand, which can happen in various ways, such as when a blade bounces from an imperfect parry. Some weapons, such as many later sabre designs, combine the knuckle bow and hand guard into a single 'shell guard', which offers excellent hand protection at the cost of fairly large size. The knuckle bow can also be used to punch at close quarters.

It is possible to trace the evolution of hand protection through a series of weapons. The medieval arming sword had only a simple crosspiece in many cases, which was entirely sufficient if the user was wearing an armoured gauntlet. Similar swords were carried for self-defence by gentlemen who would not be wearing armour or carrying a shield when about town, so it became desirable to augment the weapon's hand protection. This began with a few simple metal loops and gradually evolved into an elaborate system of bars and loops that made up the characteristic swept hilt of the early rapier.

The swept hilt evolved for many years. One of the quillions could be bent down to make a knuckle bow, but the usefulness of a crosspiece was such that later weapons had both knuckle protection and quillions. Eventually, the increasingly complex swept hilt was replaced by a solid cup of metal, creating the later cup-hilt rapier.

Rapier hilts were hard on clothing, wearing away expensive cloth by rubbing at it when the weapon was worn. They were also heavy and cumbersome when not in use. The rapier itself was rather long and heavy, and as fashions changed it evolved into the small-sword. This weapon featured a much smaller hand guard and a simple knuckle bow, with a single vestigial quillion remaining in many cases.

The small-sword was much lighter and easier to carry than a rapier, but offered far less protection to the user's hand. This was entirely acceptable when small-swords fought other small-swords, as they were purely thrusting weapons, and were unlikely to take fingers off. When facing a cutting sword, the lack of hand protection could be a liability.

It is possible to infer a similar evolution in hand protection through cutting weapons like the backsword and sabre, though the sabre was subject to so many influences that such an inference is not accurate. Both the backsword and sabre have similar principles underlying their hand protection, however.

The backsword is a heavy-bladed cutting sword that uses a basket hilt to fully enclose the user's hand and protect it from almost any attack, while the sabre's hand protection can vary considerably. Many weapons have only a small disc or oval-shaped hand guard and a stirrup-shaped knuckle bow. Others use a much larger and broader configuration, known as a shell-guard or coquille. This is asymmetrical, allowing the weapon to be carried comfortably in a scabbard but offering good protection to the outside of the sabreur's arm.

Other than when used to strike with, the hand protection of the sabre and backsword is passive in nature. That is to say, it is not often or readily used to bind or trap an opponent's blade. A wide shell-guard can be used in the manner of quillions against a thrust, but in a sabre-versus-sabre cutting match, the main function of hand protection is to prevent accidental or deliberate disablement of the sword hand. Similarly, there is no ricasso; the hand is entirely within the hand guard. The mode of use of such weapons is, as we shall see, quite different to the rapier, the active use of whose hand protection was an integral part of the fencing art.

The Cut and the Thrust

The cut and the thrust are, of course, the two means by which swords are primarily used to inflict harm. It is possible to punch with the quillions or knuckle bow, or to strike with the pommel, but these are expedients only. The sword is not a club, and belongs at the sharp end of the sharp–blunt continuum.

The debate about which is more effective – point or edge – has raged for as long as there have been points and edges. It has been said that 'the point is faster than the edge', and perhaps rightly so, but it is equally true that there are circumstances where the point is not easy to employ.

A thrust is made by pushing the weapon toward the opponent. In this context, the sword can be thought of as a sharp point at a finite distance from the user's hand. What is in between is not very important; a spear would be just as effective under most circumstances. In most cases the thrust is made by straightening the arm, which keeps the point (and also anything the opponent might do) as far away from the weapon's user as possible.

At least one fencing instructor is prone to saying that 'if you can keep the dangerous bit of your weapon close to the opponent and away from you, you're doing something right'. Facetious as this may sound, it is an excellent rule for thrusting swords. The length of the blade allows the point to be employed from a safe distance, and therefore a longer sword has a significant advantage – as does a tall swordsman with a long reach. However, this assumes that the opponent is content to remain at a distance where he can receive thrusts without being able to retaliate. If this were the case all the time, swords would have gone out of fashion long ago and the pike would be the ultimate hand weapon.

Often, the opponent is not at optimum distance. A swordsman can of course move to change the distance between himself and his opponent, but sometimes that distance is quite short and the thrust has to be executed with a bent arm. There are times when such an attack is the best option. Rather than extending the arm to present the point at the opponent, it may be more efficacious to hold the weapon still, relative to the body, and to move forward instead.

This is not a thrust as such, terminology purists may point out, but it drives the weapon into the target with bodyweight behind it, and can be hard to defend against. On the other hand, it deprives the thrusting-sword user of his main advantage. By extending only his arm, he could keep his body out of reach of the opponent. A close-quarters point attack made by moving the whole body forward brings the swordsman, and not just his arm, into reach of retaliation. If the opponent extends fully with a sword of similar length then the attacker will be outreached and may impale himself without his own attack landing.

An extended arm is often a good form of defence as well as attack. The threatening point prevents the opponent from moving in, while the blade and hand protection create a cone-shaped area into which the opponent's sword cannot reach. Not coincidentally, this cone protects the only part of the attacker that is within reach – his arm. A cut at the sword arm will likely hit the weapon's hand protection and will be ineffective.

There are drawbacks to the thrust, however. A thrust moves down a straight line. If the defender is not on that line for any reason, the thrust will fail entirely and may leave the attacker exposed to a counter-attack. If the defender sidesteps or otherwise dodges a thrust, or the attacker's aim is off, then nothing is achieved.

It is surprisingly hard to launch a clean thrust at an opponent who is moving, and the attacker's body mechanics must also be good if he is to put the point where he intends to. The point is at the end of an extended arm and the length of a blade, so even a small angle can result in a miss. If the attacker's body mechanics are incorrect, resulting in tension in his body, a thrust that is well aimed at its start can be dragged off target before it arrives.

A thrust is also relatively easy to deflect. Almost anything can push aside a thrust, not least because of the leverage available against a long blade and extended arm. Weapons can be used to parry, but even a sharp-edged blade can be deflected with a bare hand if the defender pushes against the flat of the weapon. Grabbing a sharp blade is not advisable without an armoured glove, however.

The thrust is thus a rather committed action, and must land cleanly with forward motion to have any effect. A point that lands 'flat', i.e. is moving sideways when it strikes the target, may well fail to penetrate or could inflict only a shallow surface wound. Thrusts are particularly difficult to land in the chaos of a melee, where opponents may be very close and there is little room to set up a clean thrust. Against this is balanced the fact that almost any penetration of the torso will cause a very severe, probably disabling or even fatal, injury.

It is also worth mentioning that a thrust can be made by simply pushing the weapon forward. It requires no momentum of the blade. Indeed, it is possible that an opponent may impale himself by rushing forward onto a point aimed at him. This is, again, not a thrust as such, as the sword is static and the opponent supplies the force, but the effects are equally disastrous for the target.

The cut can be executed in two ways, both of which work under the right circumstances. A slashing cut, which relies on the sharpness of the blade to slice the target's flesh, is made by bringing the edge into contact and then moving it with pressure against the target, causing the blade to slice. Such cuts can be made subtly and with great finesse, requiring little more than wrist movement.

Heavier, hacking cuts are made from the elbow or, more commonly, from the shoulder. This is a very graphic movement and quite easy for an opponent to 'read' and prepare to parry. Heavy blows of this sort are also liable to smash through a weak parry, though they do open up the attacker for retaliation to a much greater extent than slashing cuts tend to. Light cuts can be delivered with the arm held in a good defensive position, with the hand guard covering many possible lines of counter-attack and denying them to the opponent. Light slashing cuts are not excessively committed, allowing the swordsman to remain well prepared for defence and in good control of his weapon.

Heavy, hacking cuts require that the weapon move a lot more in order to develop momentum, and usually take it out of its defensive position. A counter-attack at this moment is likely to succeed, though one that is made too late may not prevent both swordsmen from hitting one another.

Some heavy swords can shear right through a limb or even decapitate an opponent on a hacking blow, and a properly executed heavy cut that bites deep and then is drawn to slice can be devastating. However, heavy cuts are not necessarily more damaging than slashes, especially when made with a fairly light sword.

Heavy cuts are instinctive, and thus tend to be used by swordsmen under grave pressure or when involved in the chaos of a melee. Since they make use of much of the body rather than just the sword arm, they are also easier to deliver. A fatigued sword arm can force the most skilled swordsman to cease making neat, controlled slashes in favour of whole-body-driven hacks. Someone who is this tired needs to win soon or he will become very vulnerable – but if one of these blows lands it may end the matter then and there.

To some extent, cuts are a defence as well as an attack. A blade that is whirling around the user's head passes through several lines in which an opponent may attack, and can – deliberately or otherwise – deflect an incoming cut or thrust. Some styles of swordsmanship make use of this, delivering cuts in such a way that the moving sword closes off some lines of attack along the way.

As a result of the way they move, cuts are likely to strike the outer parts of the body – the arms and perhaps the head, or the outside of the torso where there is significant protection from muscles and ribs. Skin is also surprisingly thick, and a thick coat can sometimes defeat a cut where a thrust would probably punch through clothing and skin. The bones of the skull might be sufficient protection against a light cut, though the results would not be pretty and the same cut on the neck would kill more or less immediately.

Overall, cuts are less likely to hit a vital part of the opponent and may not penetrate deeply enough to kill straight away. They will, however, weaken the opponent by bleeding, pain and slashed muscles or tendons, so even if it is not possible to deliver a good, clean cut that will kill outright, the opponent may be placed in a position where he has to surrender or can be easily finished off.

The danger space for a thrust is a long but very narrow one. If the target is anywhere else at the time of the thrust then the attack will fail. On the other hand, the cut lacks reach but travels in an arc, and anything on that arc is in danger. The cut needs to land edge first, and there are some points in the arc where the cut is very weak, but a sharp-edged blade is a serious threat at any point in its movement. It is not unreasonable to say that while a thrust is more likely to kill an opponent in a single attack, it is also harder to land cleanly. A cut is less likely to instantly stop an opponent, but it will probably achieve at least a weakening wound.

It would be excessively simplistic to declare that thrusts are better in a 'duel' situation and at longer distance, and cuts are ideal for close-quarters work and the chaos of a melee, but this not a bad rule of thumb most of the time. If two swordsmen with equal-length cut-and-thrust swords square off and one takes his weapon off line to begin a cut, his opponent should be able to thrust at him before the cut lands. It is fair to say that in this case 'the point is quicker than the edge'. However, once a few blows have been struck and the fencers are moving around, there will be situations where it is quicker and more effective to make a fast slash than to attempt a thrust.

Thus the point-versus-edge debate has remained unresolved to this day, and in reality the only constant rule is that providing the weapon has both a point and an edge, then each has its place and the skilled swordsman should be able not only to attack effectively with both but also to make an informed decision about which is best under the current circumstances. To be wedded to either is to pass up opportunities that might otherwise present themselves.

The Art of Defence

The term 'fencing' comes from 'defence', which may seem counter-intuitive. Is not the purpose of armed combat to disable or kill the opponent? It is, of course, but a victory won at the price of a mortal wound is not worth much. There are cultures that indoctrinate their warriors with a disregard for life, including their own, which can create formidable fighters. However, this can be taken too far.

A swordsman who is killed in his first fight, whether or not he slays his opponent, is of no further fighting value. Even if his life as an individual is considered to be worthless, he represents a significant investment in terms of training and equipment, which is wasted if he flings away his life in an all-out attack.

Ironically, perhaps, aggression can function as a form of defence. An opponent who is forced onto the defensive is less likely to land a blow of his own, and a sufficiently determined assault may well find a way through his defence. It requires more skill and precision to defend than to attack, so a tired or outmatched swordsman might be well advised to go on the offensive and try to win rather than gambling on parrying the blows of a superior opponent.

However, a swordsman who is overly aggressive or who just predictably flails away will be destroyed by a cool-headed and skilled opponent, so in practice aggression must be tempered with caution. A sudden violent assault is a useful tactical gambit, but done constantly it is exhausting and predictable.

A skilled swordsman thus flows between attack and defence, and it can be hard to see where one ends and the other begins. An opponent can be kept from attacking effectively by the constant threat of a swordsman's blade. This can be in the form of spoiling attacks; essentially the swordsman makes an attack expecting it to be parried or avoided. If the opponent does not deal with the attack, he is hit. If he does successfully defend, the swordsman is not unduly worried. He has prevented his opponent from attacking and not compromised himself by staking too much on a low-percentage attack.

Feints can also be used in this manner. A feint attack is one that is not real, and is distinct from a real attack that is not the swordsman's final intention or that is a spoiling movement intended mainly to prevent the opponent from developing his own attack. Depending on the opponent, a feint can be as subtle as a shifting of balance or the movement of a foot, or it can be a big, graphic wind-up for a massive blow, which 'telegraphs' the swordsman's intention. Of course, he wants the opponent to see what is coming and react accordingly, because he intends to do something else.

A feint can be used to keep the opponent guessing whether or not the swordsman is going to attack at all, or it can be used to set up an attack by drawing the opponent's guard to cover where he expects the attack to be going. It can also be converted to a real attack if the opponent disregards it or simply fails to see it.

Feinting can be overused or used inappropriately. It is possible to feint an attack in the hope of drawing the opponent's weapon out of position and then cutting or thrusting somewhere else, only to find that he has not reacted. In this case, the feint attack, had it been taken to completion, might have succeeded. This can happen because the swordsman fails to 'sell' the feint to the opponent, because the opponent fails to recognise it, or because the opponent has become used to the swordsman's habit of feinting and simply ignores his first blade motion in any exchange.

Any feint must be performed 'with open eyes', as the saying goes, i.e. the swordsman must watch for his opponent's reaction and decide whether to abort his movement, turn the feint into a real attack, or proceed with his intended action if the feint has succeeded. Some opponents will panic and blindly lash out when attacked; a feint that draws such a response can get an unwary swordsman killed.

The use of the feint helps create ambiguity about what the swordsman is actually trying to do. Someone who has been taught the strokes and parries with a sword, but does not really understand how to fight with it, tends to make simple and obvious actions, which are easily defeated. A swordsman who constantly conceals his intentions, sometimes attacking directly, sometimes feinting and sometimes not attacking at all, is much harder to predict. Even when his intentions can be clearly read, his opponent cannot be sure that he is not, in effect, telling lies.

As already noted, it is generally easier to attack than to defend. However, if an opponent's attack can be successfully defended against, it becomes much simpler to hit him. This is in part because he has to come into range to strike – so the swordsman has less distance to cover to reach his opponent – and in part because he is already committed to an action, so the swordsman knows what the opponent is doing and will likely do next.

Of course, in order to make a useful counter-attack the swordsman has to survive. He can hope that the opponent misses, but this is not a viable strategy in most cases. Alternatively, he can defend with a parry or he can try to avoid the attack. Thrusts can be deflected with the unarmed hand or with a weapon or object held in either hand. Cuts cannot be satisfactorily stopped with flesh; some kind of parrying implement is necessary.

Parries are normally made with the true edge of the blade close to the hand guard (i.e. the forte), and must be wide and strong enough to ensure that the opponent's attack does not strike home. It is relatively easy to deflect a thrust; cuts require a more solid parry. In either case the 'principle of defence' used in a great many fencing systems is that the foible (weak part) of the opponent's blade should be opposed with the forte (strong part) of the defender's.

If a successful parry is made, it becomes possible to riposte. This is an attack made after a successful parry, and takes advantage of the fact that the opponent has committed himself. If a good, controlled parry is made, then a fast riposte is probably the most certain of all attempts to strike the opponent. The window of opportunity is short, however; the opponent will in most cases either follow up his attack or retire out of range.

The parry-riposte can be used deliberately to hit an otherwise tricky opponent. A skilled swordsman can take advantage of the fact that his opponent has developed a high level of skill at this technique by making a not-totally-committed (but convincing) attack that he knows the opponent will parry. Most properly trained swordsmen have a riposte reflex; when they feel the blades make contact they will launch an immediate and rapid riposte. A more skilled opponent can take advantage of this by drawing this riposte, parrying it in turn and then launching a counter-riposte.

Thus an opponent who is clever and tricky on the attack can be made predictable by drawing his well-trained reflexive riposte. This sort of second-intention fencing is more the stuff of sporting matches and formal duels than battlefield melees, but it is what sets excellent swordsmen apart from merely well-trained ones.

Instead of parrying, it is possible to use a 'void' to defeat an attack. This is a movement that leaves empty space (a void) where the swordsman was. The simplest form of void is a sidestep or slight retreat to make the attack fall short, but there are some highly acrobatic voids incorporated into certain fighting systems.

Of course, a void alone is not an effective defence any more than a parry is. If the opponent's attack is defeated but he is not at least threatened with a counter of some kind, he will simply follow up with more attacks. Voids are thus usually accompanied by a counter-attack of some sort, often a stop-cut or stop-thrust.

Stop-hits, as the name suggests, are intended to stop the opponent or his weapon arm from moving towards the target. For example, a swordsman might avoid a cut by moving just out of reach and cut at the opponent's arm rather than parrying. The blow to the arm will ideally disable the opponent, but even if it does not it should serve to deflect or halt the cut. A very sharp-pointed sword will not stop an opponent immediately of course; he will cease moving forward only after the stop-thrust has penetrated a certain distance. For this reason, stop-hits are risky when performed without an accompanying void.

Distance can also be used to the swordsman's advantage. Often termed 'measure', the distance between two opponents determines whether or not they can reach one another to hit, and what sort of movement will be required to do so. Fighting at very close measure, where it is possible to simply cut or thrust at the opponent and land a hit, is very risky, as it allows little time for reaction to whatever the opponent does. Conversely, at a very long measure it will be necessary to make an obvious movement to close in, which will indicate the intention to attack.

It has been wisely said that the only reasons for being close enough to an opponent to hit are because you intend to hit him or you want him to try to hit you. Closing in can be used to draw an attack, and measure can be used very subtly by a skilled swordsman. By hovering just at the outer limits of his opponent's reach he can goad the opponent into making an attack while giving himself as much time as possible to react with a parry or void. This is a risk of course, but the art of fencing is at least in part about balancing the risk of being hit against the chance to strike a telling blow.

Measure translates to time, but not equally for all weapons and opponents. A long measure translates to plenty of time to see what the opponent is doing and to react, but this is relative to the speed with which a given swordsman can move and the characteristics of his weapon. A thrust with a long sword may well cross the same amount of distance in a shorter time than a cut from a heavier weapon.

By constantly moving, a swordsman can create ambiguity about his intentions and where he is going to be at any given moment in the future. Since any attack takes a finite amount of time to complete, uncertainty about whether the target is going to be where the attack is aimed can cause an opponent to simply abort it. Measure can of course be used actively, stepping back out of reach ('defending with measure') when an opponent attacks or moving in close to pressurise an opponent who likes to fight at long measure.

Movement is typically accomplished by a shuffle movement, whereby the feet do not cross. Whichever foot is forward in the system being used stays forward when moving in this manner. Steps are short, and maintain good balance and the ability to stop or change direction at need. Similar movements can be used to travel diagonally or to circle around an opponent.

If the feet cross over, this is termed a pass. Passing is used to change stance in some systems, moving from an offensively oriented posture with the weapon hand forward to a defensively oriented one with the off-hand forward. It can also be used to cover ground quickly or to launch a long attack.

The lunge is also used to cover ground on an attack. It is accomplished by driving forward using the back foot and allowing the front one to move forward. Some systems use very long lunges, some shorter ones, and some do not include the lunge at all. In addition to covering distance yet allowing a rapid recovery out of reach of a counter-attack, the lunge also generates tremendous force and can drive a thrust right through an opponent.

The art of defence, then, can be summed up as 'hitting without being hit'. The key to this, to a great extent, is control. Control of one's own weapon, control of measure, and to some extent control of the opponent's actions. This can seem impossible to the novice swordsman, but with proper training and experience it becomes habitual. Every sword weapon – indeed, every hand weapon in existence – has certain 'lines of attack'. These are not arbitrarily made up; they are determined by biomechanics and the characteristics of the sword.

Perhaps the most instinctive line of attack for a cutting weapon is the downward forehand stroke towards the head and neck area. This is a movement that the human body is well configured to make, and exploits the additional momentum of the weapon due to gravity. A horizontal backhand cut at the ribs is another obvious line of attack.

By studying the mechanics of attacks with a sword, it is possible to discern several obvious lines. There will always be some variation, but these lines serve as a broad guide to where an attack might come from. Additional information can be gained from how the opponent is holding his weapon, and also what it is feasible for him to do from that position.

A suicidally reckless or totally incompetent opponent might be highly unpredictable, but even the most crazed attacker is unlikely to make an attack that will obviously fail. Reaching in with a deep cut to the legs, leaving the head exposed to a counter-attack, is unlikely to be much more than assisted suicide under many circumstances. Similarly, cutting into a line that is already blocked by the opponent's sword seems a little pointless.

Thus, although a novice swordsman may feel horribly vulnerable, in fact he can severely limit his opponent's options by adopting a guard position that covers some of the likely lines of attack. Knowing which lines are impractical allows the opponent's attacks to be predicted, though obviously if he is skilled he may feint into an 'open' line to draw a parry and then attack elsewhere.

In order to avoid the possibility of a sudden reckless thrust, most swordsmen are trained to keep their blades 'in opposition' as much as possible. Essentially this means that the opponent cannot hit by simply moving his weapon towards the target. If the blades are blocking one another in this manner, they are said to be in engagement (or simply engaged), and the line of attack is closed. Normally the true edges are turned towards one another when the weapons are engaged.

To get into an open line, a swordsman will use a movement termed a disengage. This does not mean moving away out of combat; it is the term for passing around the opponent's blade from a closed or closing line to one that is open or opening. In many systems, 'disengage' also applies to a specific circular motion of the blade used to accomplish the move into an open line, but that usage is not universal. The disengage movement can be used against a static blade, or against one that is closing the line in which the swordsman wishes to attack. Changing the line in this manner to avoid a parry is termed deceiving the parry.

It is possible to control an opponent's actions not only by limiting his options but by offering him one. By deliberately allowing the guard position to drift a little and creating an opening, a skilled swordsman can tempt his opponent into making just the attack he is hoping for, then parry or void it and counter while the opponent is committed.

Another way to control the opponent is to gain control of his blade. There are essentially three ways that this can be done. The first is to attack the blade, i.e. to strike it in order to push it aside. The most obvious option is to simply bash it with a weapon, essentially making a cut but against the blade rather than the opponent. Heavy-handed attacks on the blade can be easy for the opponent to spot and to deceive, moving his weapon out of the way and then counter-attacking before the swordsman can recover to a well-guarded position. Although unscientific and rather obvious, this technique, sometimes termed a 'batter', can be highly effective.

The commonest attack on the blade is the beat, which is a sharp rap on the blade, but it is also possible to make a grazing beat (termed a glissade in many systems), retaining pressure on the blade and sliding up it after contact, then coming off just in time to land a thrust. A beat can also be used to provoke a reaction – a nervous opponent may reflexively parry when his blade is beaten, allowing a final action in a different line before he can recover.

Instead of being attacked, the blade can instead be taken, i.e. pushed or carried to a different position. Simple pressure against the blade can work, though this is more likely to provoke a reaction such as a disengage than to succeed in its own right. More effectively, a bind can be used. This is the origin of the figure of speech 'in a bind', and is usually accomplished by locking the foible of the opponent's blade between forte and hand guard, using the quillions if the weapon has them. A bind very strongly controls the opponent's blade and will often allow an attack to be made without any danger of a counter-attack.

The final way to control an opponent's blade is to seize it or his weapon arm. Grabbing a sharp weapon is not a good idea unless metal hand protection is in use, but many swords can be seized in the unarmed or 'off' hand and held immobile or pulled from the user's grasp. The sword arm can also be seized, either to control the weapon or to drag the opponent into an attack.

Most disarming techniques are based upon seizures of some kind, though usually it is a combination of weapon and unarmed hand that is used to disarm the opponent. Many sword combat systems also include a certain amount of wrestling and kicking; a sword fight is not always an elegant 'conversation of the blades', and the ability to wrestle can make all the difference in a desperate encounter.

Historically, the subtleties of swordsmanship were more commonly observed in a formal one-on-one encounter or in 'salle fencing', i.e. training or sporting matches, than in open combat. On the battlefield, success tended to be a matter of moving evasively, timing attacks well and forcing opponents onto the defensive with judicious aggression. Attacks, parries and ripostes tended to be fairly simple, though a skilled swordsman could still make use of his entire repertoire of technique if the occasion arose.

In a more formal one-on-one situation, there were often rules and niceties about what could and could not be done, or at least what was 'bad form'. At times, social conventions prevailed whereby gentlemen were expected to fight duels over the most ridiculous of pretexts, but would be hanged if they killed their opponent. In such a situation, skill was more important than ever – it is actually harder to deliver a disabling wound that will not be mortal than it is to kill someone with a sword – and techniques for disarming the opponent, or pummelling him into submission, were an excellent way of avoiding a victory that would lead to the gallows.

CHAPTER 2

The Empire and the Arena: The Roman Gladius

The Roman Empire grew from a single city state into a multi-city republic and finally a vast empire that dominated Europe as well as parts of Africa and the Middle East. It is not unreasonable to say that this empire was created and protected by legions of heavy infantrymen whose primary armament was the gladius, a short stabbing sword.

However, the popular image of Roman legions, with every man uniformly equipped and armed with pila (javelins), a large shield and a short stabbing sword, is at best only partially correct. Equipment varied somewhat, and the gladius was not the only sword found in Roman hands.

The military forces of Rome spanned a period from around 750 BC to AD 476, and even after that a part of the empire lived on in the form of the Byzantine Empire. Naturally, armament and fighting styles changed with time, region and the nature of the opposition. By the time the empire was in its heyday, its forces had to be able to deal with a wide range of opponents. This was a very different situation from the early days, when Rome's enemies were rather more local.

In the later part of the Roman era, the eastern and western parts of the empire were essentially separate, with their own rulers and differing military systems that had diverged from the classical legions that are most familiar to us. The Eastern Roman Empire, in its form as the Byzantine Empire, largely relied on heavily armoured cavalry rather than the infantry-based legions of the early Imperial Roman period.

Even within those classical legions, uniformity of equipment was less common than popular depictions might indicate. While weaponry had to be uniform in order to make the Roman style of combat work, protective equipment varied considerably. Helmet design changed over the years, but a helmet of older design that could be refurbished and returned to service would be kept. Some legionaries probably wore equipment that was older than their grandfather.

Similarly, although the legions are usually depicted in uniform armour made up of laminated metal strips, in fact soldiers also wore mail and scale armour, or sometimes a breastplate. Men in the same unit might have different armour, not least because it was expensive to produce and what mattered was protecting soldiers, not making them look alike.

The original forces of Rome were organised much like those of the Greek city states, and were formed of a spear-armed phalanx supported by lesser units. Military service was on a militia or civic-duty basis, which meant that any force was composed of citizen-soldiers rather than professionals who would be under arms long enough to receive extensive training.

The richest and most influential citizens formed the backbone of the army, as citizens had to provide their own armour and weapons. These men were equipped much like Greek hoplites, with a long spear, large shield and varying amounts of armour. A rich man might be able to afford a breastplate, a helmet and greaves to protect his lower legs. Most of the rest of him was covered by his shield.

Less well-off men might have only partial armour, and those who could not afford the long spear and large shield served in lighter-equipped units on the flanks. This system was reasonably well suited to the inter-polis (city state versus city state) warfare of Ancient Greece, but proved less effective against the tribes of hilly Italy.

A phalanx needs fairly level ground to be effective, and if both sides are equipped this way then they have to choose a battle site suited to the strengths of both opponents. A differently equipped force need not do so, perhaps forcing the phalanx to fight in terrain that negates its main asset – an impenetrable wall of spear points – by breaking it up.

Under such circumstances, the long spear is not as effective as its wielders might like, and Roman phalangites were forced to take to their swords in close combat. These weapons were also derived from Greek traditions, and were cutting swords very similar in design to the Greek kopis. Indeed, there have been suggestions that the kopis actually had its origins with the Etruscan people of Italy and was adopted by the Greeks rather than the other way around.

Either way, the early Roman citizen-soldier was equipped with a single-handed, single-edged sword whose blade was angled forward, and bellied out to concentrate mass at the striking point. The curve of the blade also assisted with a drawn cut, making this a very deadly weapon in skilled hands. Exactly how skilled the Roman hands that wielded it were is a matter for debate, as citizen-soldiers did not receive formal military training. That said, a rich man who knew he had a duty to fight at need might well arrange for at least some basic instruction with his weapons.

Rome gradually increased in power, becoming influential in Italy at the head of what was essentially an alliance of city states. Forces were arranged into 'legions' but these were not the legions we normally think of today; those came later, after major reforms of the Roman military system.

Around 400 BC, Celtic tribes began pushing into Italy across the Alps. Rome and her allies resisted them, leading to a graphic demonstration of the weakness of the Roman phalanx system. In battle close to the River Allia, the Celts threw the main weight of their attack against the weak flanking units, routing them. The central, more heavily equipped phalanx was then surrounded and ground down, depriving Rome of many of her leading citizens as well as her main fighting force. As a result, Rome was occupied and largely sacked.

This defeat, along with others in war with Italian tribes, forced Rome to reorganise her army. The Greek-style phalanx was abandoned in favour of a far more flexible arrangement that allowed tactical manoeuvres and paved the way for the classic legions.

The new Roman army was organised into maniples, typically of 120 men each. These were subdivided by experience and armament. The Velites were light troops who screened the main force, throwing javelins at the enemy and then withdrawing behind the lines for protection. These were the least experienced men, who would eventually move into the main infantry force to be replaced by new recruits.

The main force was organised as three lines. The young Hastati formed the first line and the more experienced Principes the second. These lines were formed in a 'chequerboard' pattern, with units of the second line able to move forward and support or relieve the Hastati as needed. If things went well, these two lines would be sufficient to win a battle, with the Hastati engaging first and gaining battle experience, and the Principes getting involved when their greater steadiness was needed.

A third line, formed of the most experienced men and named Triarii, was formed in maniples of sixty men rather than the 120 of the Hastati and Principes. 'To fall back on the Triarii' was a Roman figure of speech indicating that things had become rather grim, but when the Triarii engaged they were a powerful force formed of the oldest and most experienced members of the legion.

The Hastati and Principes did away with their hoplite-style equipment and replaced it with a short sword (usually termed the gladius) and heavy javelins called pila. They retained a large shield, but its shape was altered from the round hoplon shield of the phalangite to a curved rectangular shape. This created the scutum shield, which was characteristic of the Roman legionary thereafter.

The Triarii retained their hoplite-style equipment for a time, but eventually converted to the same arms and armour as the Hastati and Principes. This made the Roman military system highly unusual, in that the sword was the primary battlefield weapon of its infantry rather than a sidearm as was the case in many other forces.

Evolution of the army was inevitable. As Roman power increased, the military burden placed on its citizens grew ever larger. The richest citizens formed the main fighting force, as they were the only ones able to afford proper equipment. Their long absence through the campaign season – perhaps several years in a row – severely impacted the Roman economy, as their businesses and estates stood leaderless.

The legions were reorganised in 107 BC by Gaius Marius. This was part of a series of measures to overcome a desperate manpower shortage. The Senate had recently introduced a system whereby the state paid for equipment, not the soldier. This permitted recruitment from the poorer echelons of Roman society, who were rewarded with regular pay and the promise of land when they retired. Rather than raising a legion when needed and disbanding it afterwards, a professional army was thus created. Long-service troops could be drilled and trained when not on campaign, raising the effectiveness of the legions considerably.

Under the Marian reforms, the divisions between Hastati, Principes and Triarii no longer existed; all soldiers became legionaries and equal in status. The Velites were done away with, and the legion of ten maniples, each containing these various types of troops, became one of ten more homogenous cohorts.

The Marian legion had ten cohorts, each of six centuries. These contained eighty men rather than the 100 implied by the name, making 480 legionaries in a cohort, and 4,800 in a legion. A legion would be supported by lighter units, usually supplied as auxiliary forces by allies or raised in areas controlled by Rome, but the Roman legion itself fought as heavy infantry. The standard tactic was to form up the cohorts in three lines, engaging as needed or moving out to flank the enemy or to exploit a tactical advantage.

Marius introduced (or at least standardised) training methods for the new-style legions. Men spent long hours cutting and stabbing at a wooden post or training with double-weight weapons. This increased their individual stamina in combat, but the endurance of a force as a whole was also improved by drill and organisation.

At need, Roman troops could close their ranks and create a solid wall of shields, but they normally fought with a reasonable amount of space around each man. A legionary had enough room to move around a little as needed but was trained to be mindful of his neighbours and to help them out when necessary. Rather than attacking the opponent in front of him, the Roman soldier was often able to make an attack from the flank on the enemy warrior facing his neighbour, increasing the effectiveness of each legionary by teamwork.

The effectiveness of the Roman sword was enhanced in other ways, too. The standard tactic was to hurl pila just before contact with an enemy force, then charge (or countercharge) to take advantage of the disruption caused by the hail of javelins. What then ensued was close combat, in which the sword and shield were used in combination.

The Roman gladius was not a 'fencing' sword; it was a battlefield killing tool. Many of the techniques used by the legionary employed sword and shield in conjunction, with the shield used to bash and drive back an opponent or to pin his weapon arm. The Roman army recognised that a soldier, no matter how well conditioned by his training, only remained effective for so long. Drills were created whereby a tiring man could swap out of the front line and be replaced by his well-rested comrade, regaining his breath ready to move back in when needed. Wounded men could also be pulled out of the line before the enemy could finish them off.

In a less organised force, the individual warrior would have to fight until he won, was felled, or the tides of battle pushed him behind the front line. He would tire but probably not have the chance to recuperate, which meant that good fighters were sometimes killed through fatigue. Roman troops were replaced individually as they tired, and whole units could be switched mid-combat, creating greater sustained fighting power for the formation and increased survivability for individuals.

The primary weapon of this superb fighting force was the short sword, or gladius, and it was with this weapon that the Roman Empire was won. The gladius triumphed over the long pikes of the Greek phalanx, the slashing swords of the Gauls and the long-handled rhomphaia and falx of the Thracians. This was not due to any inherent superiority of the Roman weapon but to the combination of a fine sword and an excellent system for using it both individually and in massed combat.

Later, sometime in the middle of the first century AD, the gladius was replaced by a longer weapon known as a spatha. This was a cutting sword, probably first adopted by the cavalry to increase reach from the saddle when not using a spear. Much later in the history of the Roman Empire, the arms and equipment of the legions became less standardised, as many Roman formations were raised from barbarian people along the fringes of the empire. These forces tended to fight in their traditional manner with whatever weapons they normally used.

By this time the Roman Empire was in deep decline, and Rome itself was eventually overrun by barbarians. The Eastern Empire, with its capital at Constantinople, went its own way despite an attempt to reconquer the Western segment, and eventually developed into the Byzantine Empire, which endured for many more centuries. Byzantine forces inherited some of the Roman traditions of discipline and organisation, but used very different weapons to the Marian legions who had carved out and protected the empire in its heyday.

Roman Swords

The earliest sword-type weapons were essentially overgrown knives. They were made of bronze and were suitable for stabbing only. As sword-making techniques improved, these knives became longer. It became possible to create a weapon that had enough mass to make an effective cutting stroke and to retain its sharp edge.

The use of iron can be traced back at least as far as 1400 BC, spreading from Asia and the Middle East into Europe. Early iron weapons were rather poor – inferior to bronze in fact – and it was some time before swordsmiths could reliably produce steel that would take and retain an edge yet remain flexible enough to survive the rigours of combat.

The Iron Age began in Europe around 800 BC, shortly before the founding of Rome. Swordsmiths moved from making bronze weapons to iron or steel ones, but the designs remained the same for a time. Improved metallurgy allowed a longer blade to be fashioned, and gradual evolution produced a range of designs.

Practical experience created local preferences and wider trends in sword design. A short sword with a leaf-shaped blade, called xiphos by the Greeks, was used by Greeks and the Celtic peoples of eastern Europe, but many authorities including Xenophon believed that the cutting sword was a more effective battlefield weapon. This was especially true for mounted warriors and cavalry – Xenophon believed that the kopis or makhaira (using both terms to refer to a cutting sword) was far superior when used from horseback.

Meanwhile, the early Roman forces were fighting with long spears and falling back on their sidearm, a curved weapon similar to the kopis or falcata, at close quarters. These heavy-bladed cutting swords could deliver a powerful cut that might disable an opponent with a single stroke, and even on a marginal hit their curved blades would deliver a slashing cut that might weaken an enemy or force him to retreat.

To differentiate from the later gladius hispaniensis, this early sword is often now referred to as a falcata, although that term is of fairly recent origin. It is not clear what the warriors of early Rome would have called their weapons, though 'gladius' ('sword') seems likely. In any case, the early Roman sword was a reasonable compromise between an individual's sidearm and a battlefield weapon for use in massed combat. Its powerful stroke was fairly easy to deliver, requiring relatively little training to become effective, and even without a shield it could be used well.

The main drawback of a weapon of this kind is that a cutting stroke requires a fair amount of movement in order to deliver, which can disrupt the use of the shield, especially if troops are in close order. The latter was probably not that much of a problem for the early legions; when in close order, their primary weapon was the spear. If the spear became ineffective this was usually because the formation had become disordered, creating circumstances where the sword was in its element.

Forces armed in this manner fought the early wars of Roman expansion, notably against the Celts who sacked Rome around 400 BC. These favoured long cutting swords as a personal weapon, so battles of this era tended to match similarly armed men against one another once combat became personal rather than formation-versus-formation.

Expansion into Iberia brought Roman forces into contact with what they called the Celtiberians. Celtic migrations had created a mix of local and Celtic tribes, and some that were somewhere in between, throughout much of Iberia. Although the Celts elsewhere favoured cutting swords and the Iberians had made very good use of the falcata, a local design of short stabbing sword had emerged which impressed the Romans greatly.

Indeed, the Roman military were so impressed with this Spanish sword (or gladius hispaniensis) that they adopted it for general issue. This necessitated a move to a new style of swordsmanship built around the close-quarters thrust. The short, stabbing thrust was well suited to sword-and-shield combat, and to fighting in a formation. Wild swings with a long sword could endanger a soldier's comrades; thrusting was less likely to do so.

The gladius proved extremely effective and well suited to the Roman style of combat. It was equally at home in the ranks of a massed legion or in the close-quarters scramble of an assault on a fortified place or a boarding action at sea. The short sword might have been disadvantaged against longer weapons, especially the massed pikes of the Greek and Macedonian armies, but this was offset by the use of supporting weapons as well as flexible tactics.

The Roman practice of hurling pila just before contact caused significant disruption in an enemy force, creating gaps that Roman soldiers could force their way into. A spear- or pike-armed force that could not bring its massed spear points to bear was at a severe disadvantage, and this is how Roman legions decisively defeated Greek-style phalanxes when they met. A combination of using rough terrain to break up the phalanx and pila to create disorder at the critical moment of contact allowed the legionaries to fight on their own terms and to maximise the advantages offered by their short, handy swords.

Those swords were of extremely high quality, with flexible blades that would survive hard use yet retain a good edge. The steel for the blade was produced in a bloomery furnace, which could not achieve temperatures high enough to fully melt iron ore. This made creating steel a rather laborious process, and produced strips of metal that were pattern-welded together to create a composite blade.

The shortness (50–60 cm) of the gladius blade meant that it suffered relatively little stress on impact and was more likely to punch through armour than to skid off or flex as a longer blade might. This increased durability and lethality, though at the price of a shorter reach. The latter could be compensated for by technique to a great extent, but it did mean that the Roman soldier at times had to press forward rather standing in a neat shield wall.

Roman legions did sometimes use the shield wall tactic, but generally fought in a more flexible manner where each man was free to push a little ahead or to move side to side. Constant training ensured that he did not lose track of his comrades and get too far out of formation. This ability to undertake tactical movement enabled the individual Roman soldier to reach and attack an opponent who tried to hang back and turn the superior length of his weapon to his advantage.

In a less well-drilled force the unit as a whole might lose its cohesion if men moved around too much, turning the battle into a number of individual melees. The Roman system was designed in part to prevent this by ensuring a balance between flexibility and cohesion on an individual and unit level. A parallel could be drawn between a sword blade and a Roman fighting formation – both needed hardness to strike but flexibility to remain intact.

The use of the sword as a primary battlefield weapon is unusual; most forces in the ancient world were armed with axes, maces, spears or other 'battlefield' weapons, such as halberds, as their primary armament, reserving the sword or dagger for use as a sidearm. Roman forces even carried their weapons in an unusual manner; the gladius was worn on the right side and drawn vertically rather than across the body from the left. This enabled the legionary to draw his sword without interfering with the use of his shield, which might be important, since the sword was often only drawn when the enemy was very close.

Pila were thrown from a distance of about 15–20 m, a distance that it does not take long for a charging man to cross. A legionary who threw his pilum either to break up an oncoming charge or to cause disruption in an enemy force as he charged (or both) had only seconds to deploy his sword before contact. During those seconds his shield was still in play and offering good protection.

The gladius was one of the standard weapons used by gladiators – indeed, the name gladiator comes from 'swordsman', suggesting that the earliest gladiators were armed with swords of some kind. Various swords were used by different types of gladiator, along with a variety of other weapons. Some of these were fanciful or exotic, intended to give the crowd a good show with plenty of variety. For this reason, and simple tradition, the gladius hispaniensis remained in service as a gladiatorial weapon after its replacement in military service.

The gladius hispaniensis remained in mainstream military service from around 200 BC to sometime in the first century AD. After this it was replaced by the longer (60- to 80-cm) spatha. This probably started out as a cavalry weapon, perhaps derived from the cutting swords of Gaulish cavalry encountered from 100 BC onwards.

The spatha offered a horseman an extension to his reach and the ability to deliver a mighty blow with the mass of a moving horse behind it. Its adoption thus made perfect sense for cavalry, but for the infantry it required a shift in fighting styles to accommodate cutting blows with a longer weapon. Nevertheless, it was clearly very effective.

The spatha would not have supplanted the gladius if it were not at least as useful in combat. Re-equipping the legions and retraining personnel were lengthy and expensive undertakings, even though they took place on a gradual basis over many years. Had a need not been perceived, the Roman authorities – who were always concerned about efficiency – would not have authorised the changeover.

Thus the gladius hispaniensis had a relatively short career compared with the lifetime of the Roman Republic and Empire – shorter, at least, than many people believe. Yet it was extremely influential. The empire it served conquered countless tribes as well as other states, which were in some cases very powerful. It was this sword that was in the hands of the legions as Rome moved from being an important republic to a huge empire, and thus was the instrument of enormous changes that are still felt today.

The Gladius in Combat

The gladius had little hand protection, but this was not really necessary, since it was primarily used in conjunction with armour and a shield. Its blade was designed primarily for thrusting, but had sufficient mass to deliver a powerful cut. Indeed, there are accounts of limb amputations and decapitations inflicted with this weapon.

The primary attack with the gladius was an upward thrust between the ribs or under them, with the blade held horizontally. This ensured that it would slide between ribs and penetrate deeply, not that a huge penetration was necessary; a quarter of the 60-cm blade was easily sufficient to ensure a killing blow. The wide blade resulted in an equally wide wound track, which translated to a great deal of bleeding and a good chance of finding a vital organ.

The gladius was used from what is often referred to as a 'defensive' stance, i.e. with the shield side forward. This is universal in sword-and-shield fighting styles, for obvious reasons. The shield was an integral part of the fighting style, and was used for more than passive defence. Most obviously, a shield could be used to bash the opponent, causing him to stagger back and opening him up for a thrust, or to pin the opponent's sword arm by pushing against him, again making him very vulnerable.

The shield also informed the style of swordsmanship taught to Roman soldiers. It left few targets open to an attacker, and unless he had a long weapon, such as a rhomphaia, he could not reach under it to attack the legs. That left the head as the only viable target on a legionary facing his foe with his shield up. Since overhead blows with cutting weapons were inevitable, Roman helmets and armour were optimised to deflect them.

An opponent who lifted up his arm for an overhead strike might leave himself open to a thrust to the body, delivered by either the legionary he was fighting or a neighbouring comrade. Numerous remains have been found with this sort of wound, suggesting that it was a common gambit. Of course, the Roman had to have sufficient confidence in his protection that he would be willing to counter-attack rather than becoming defensive, but this was part of his training.

With a shield on the left arm, the swordsman's options were limited to the thrust and certain cuts. A downward diagonal backhand cut is possible over a shield, but it is somewhat awkward. Direct downward or forehand cuts are the primary options. Cuts might be delivered to the head or flank, especially in the case where an enemy had been deprived of his shield by a pilum sticking in it, or could be made to the enemy's lead leg.

The latter is a 'safe' attack to make under most circumstances. Angling the shield to meet a downward cut, the legionary crouched behind it and delivered a diagonal downward cut of his own under the shield, which prevented his opponent from seeing it. Even if the opponent expected such a cut, defending against it was difficult. This blow might or might not put the opponent out of the fight, but it would weaken him. If the legionary then straightened up and took a heavy step forward, he could bash his opponent backwards, forcing him to stumble on his injured leg and perhaps fall.

Cut-and-thrust (or thrust-and-cut) combinations were easy to make with the gladius. Its short length allowed it to be readied for a new blow very quickly. For example, if a downward diagonal cut were blocked with a shield, the gladius-armed fighter could turn his attack into a thrust by raising his elbow and pressing forward. His thrust would slide over the shield into the opponent's face. Likewise a failed thrust could be converted into an opportunistic cut more quickly than with a longer blade.

Fighting with the gladius, especially in the press of a shield line, required a good 'base'. Thrusts were made with a short stabbing motion, and cuts were equally short. There was little extension; the legionary remained behind his shield rather than reaching out to strike his opponent. He moved closer using his footwork rather than by reaching for his opponent.

A solid base was necessary to drive the point of the gladius deep into an opponent and also to withstand the collision when an enemy crashed into the legionary's shield. This might be deliberate, in the form of a shield bash, or would sometimes occur by accident. Either way, the legionary could not afford to lose his balance and be sent stumbling. He thus drilled endlessly to receive and deliver impact with his shield, bracing himself so that his enemy rebounded from his shield and was left open for a thrust alongside or over the top of it.

In short, the gladius was not a weapon for elegant fencing. It was a killing tool to be used in conjunction with a shield, and is perhaps more properly considered as half a weapon system – the other half being the legionary's distinctive scutum. The gladius is noteworthy as being perhaps the finest sword ever designed for use with the shield, and one of the few that has been used as a primary battlefield weapon. And of course, it is one of the very few military swords whose main mode of use is the thrust.

After the gladius faded from the scene, cutting swords dominated the battlefield (and also feuds, duels and random acts of violence) for over a thousand years. There are those who still believe that during the 'dark ages' after the fall of Rome, swords and swordsmanship fell into terminal decline. As we shall see, that is simply not so.

CHAPTER 3

Bright Blades in a Dark Age: The Warrior's Sword

The idea that a 'dark age' settled over Europe after the fall of the Roman Empire is persistent, but at best only partially true. Exactly when this dark age supposedly occurred depends on the viewpoint of the observer. Some believe that the Dark Ages lasted from the fall of Rome until the beginning of the Renaissance; others take a narrower view and suggest a period from around AD 500 to AD 1000.

The underlying concept is that Europe was plunged into an age of violence, turbulence and intellectual bankruptcy after the fall of Rome, from which it emerged only when Renaissance (or late-Medieval, depending on your viewpoint) scholars began to once again record their deep and important thoughts.

The dark age concept is often extended into social and military matters – basically, the idea that once Rome was gone everyone forgot how to build cities, to organise themselves and get along with one another. There is also a misconception that the conflicts that inevitably erupted during this period were fought by incompetents since the military art had clearly collapsed along with everything else.

A little research shows that this viewpoint, which is fortunately becoming less prevalent, is almost entirely incorrect. There was indeed a period of great upheaval, and much destruction, but cities continued to be built and societies continued to function. The military art, far from collapsing, evolved to meet new requirements, and eventually produced the medieval armies that dominated the Middle Ages.

Thus the view that once the 'light of Rome' went out there was nothing but violent barbarism is more than a little questionable. Civilised kingdoms emerged, and monasteries were built as Christianity spread. These great religious buildings are magnificent undertakings that could not have been constructed in a true 'dark age'.

Religious centres became the main centres for intellectual activity, while the general populace remained illiterate. This did curtail technological and social progress, but that does not necessarily translate to an era of barbarism.

Warfare was on a smaller and more personal scale in this period; few societies could muster the large armies that the Greeks, Macedonians, Persians or Romans had fielded. Warriors replaced soldiers, requiring a slightly different skill set, and battles turned more often on the actions of a few courageous men than on the manoeuvres of a wily commander.

These were hard and troubled times, in which the skills of the warrior were vital. The kingdoms that emerged did so because they won the fight for survival, a fight that in many cases began a significant time before Rome finally fell. Indeed, the 'light of Rome' had grown very dim long before the 'dark age' is generally supposed to have begun.

The last days of the Roman Empire and the period that followed were chaotic and violent, with whole tribes on the march, and this did lead to a period where much of value was destroyed. However, while the idea of filthy barbarians tearing down monuments and stabbing one another over a skin of wine may be dramatic, it is not a very accurate picture of events.

The Roman Empire tottered for many years before it fell, largely due to internal troubles that sapped its strength. During this period, Roman forces were augmented by the practice of subsidising tribes along the borders in return for military service when needed. These foederati, as they were known, included the Vandals, the Visigoths and the Franks.

The foederati became increasingly critical to defending the borders of the Roman Empire, especially as wars, rebellions and plague further reduced Roman manpower. These allied troops fought on behalf of the empire but were normally equipped with their traditional weapons; gone were the days of uniform legions right across the empire.

The foederati learned a great deal from their interactions with Rome, and retained some of their knowledge in later generations. This influenced the emergence of the kingdoms of the 'dark ages', which eventually led to the medieval period. In the interim, however, Europe had to endure a period of great upheaval.

Frankish Warriors

The main cause of this turbulent time was the arrival of the Huns from the east. Originating far off in Asia, perhaps on the northern borders of China, the Huns began pushing into Eastern Europe around AD 370. This forced the tribes they defeated to move westwards, some settling in Roman territory and some battling their neighbours for new land.

This series of collisions triggered a period known as *Volkswanderung*, essentially a series of migrations that caused whole tribal confederations to march right across Europe in search of a new home. The Western Roman Empire was too weak to resist these movements, but did at times try to make use of them by settling tribes where they could defend Roman territory.

The Hun invasion penetrated Europe as far as Gaul (France) before being turned back. The Huns were defeated in AD 451 at the Battle of the Catalaunian Fields, by a joint Roman-Visigothic army. This was to a great extent the last hurrah for the Western Roman Empire, while the Eastern Empire, based in Constantinople, remained fairly strong.

It is telling that the Visigoths fought jointly with Roman forces, and not as auxiliaries under Roman command. Similarly, while Roman forces were unable to stop the Huns from pillaging towns in northern Italy, a confederation of Germanic tribes inflicted a punishing defeat upon the Huns in AD 454. Although the Huns continued to cause problems for a time, their power was spent and they faded from the stage of history.

However, the events set in motion by the Hunnic invasion continued. Tribes, and entire confederations of tribes, migrated far from their ancestral homelands and settled in new lands. The Vandals reached Spain and set up a kingdom there before moving to North Africa. There, they became so powerful that the Eastern Roman Empire treated with them as equals.

Although the name Vandal has come to be associated with wanton destruction, the Vandals were no more or less prone to this than anyone else. Like many of the 'barbarian' tribes, they had a sophisticated culture and were capable of making objects of great beauty. Likewise, the 'barbarian' tribes that moved elsewhere in Europe took with them a rich culture and a functioning society. Once these displaced peoples were able to settle, they built cities and created kingdoms that were anything but huddles of barbarian hovels.

Some of these resettled peoples gave their names to the lands they now called home, and these regions are often still called by that name. Thus the *Volkswanderung* was in many ways the very beginning of modern Europe. The Lombards, for example, did not originate in the region now called Lombardy, but they made a home there and gave it its modern name. Likewise, the Franks were a Germanic people who crossed the Rhine into Gaul and gave the region a new identity.

The Franks were, like many of the Germanic tribal confederations, a tough and warlike people who had been displaced but retained enough fighting power to carve out a new home. They became foederati of Rome, but this was not a one-sided deal. In the past, barbarians were recruited by the powerful Roman Empire and served it. Now, the Franks aligned themselves with Rome to mutual benefit. They were not merely subjects of the Empire; their kingdom was recognised by Rome in AD 357.

The Franks fought in a manner not unlike that of the Roman legions. They may have been influenced by long years of conflict and interaction, or may have evolved their own system in parallel. Either way, Frankish warriors generally fought on foot, armed with shield and sword. Like the Roman legionaries, Franks did not favour missile weapons other than a spear or axe hurled just before contact.

The Frankish spear was a shortish but heavy design called an angon, which could be used in hand-to-hand combat or hurled into the enemy ranks just before a charge. Their 'signature weapon', however, was the francisca, or throwing axe. Hurled at close range, the axe could split a shield or kill a man, and might bounce off a glancing contact and continue on its way into the enemy force. This lethal and somewhat random weapon gained a terrifying reputation among the enemies of the Franks.

Once his throwing weapon was gone, the Frankish warrior engaged with sword and shield. The techniques for using a long cutting sword with a shield are different to those associated with the short stabbing sword, and will be considered later in this chapter.

The Franks succeeded in unifying Gaul under the rule of the Merovingian dynasty, which ruled for almost three centuries before being supplanted by the Carolingian dynasty. Although at times fragmented, the Frankish kingdoms dominated what had been Gaul, and created a Frankish empire.

In the 730s, the Franks were able to repel the Moorish invasion coming into Europe by way of the Pyrenees. The Moors had previously seemed unbeatable, but were turned back in a series of battles in south-western France. This had powerful implications for the future of Christianity in Europe, and the force that achieved it was not some benighted barbarian host but the army of an organised kingdom.

This kingdom, and others like it, built cities and had a complex social structure. An increasingly powerful Church influenced kings and nobles, and some prominent Church officials became important war leaders as well. The feudal system that gradually emerged became the basis for most European societies for centuries to come. It was based on a system of duties, whereby each social stratum received benefits from those above and had duties to them.

Of course, the feudal system was biased towards those who had wealth and power, but it provided a stable base, which allowed a measure of prosperity at least some of the time. This permitted population growth, which in turn increased the power of the society as a whole. The feudal system supported an elite military class who trained at arms and were well equipped with the best weaponry available.

Numbers in a force were filled out by levies, who were rather less well equipped and trained. Thus it tended to be the actions of the elite that decided a battle rather than the tactics of an integrated and homogenous force. In the relatively small armies of the era, this system worked well enough that those with the best-equipped and most skilled warrior class became dominant.

Viking Warriors

It is common to refer to the Scandinavians, or Norsemen, of the 'Dark Ages' as Vikings, but while this is a useful label it is not very accurate. The term Viking refers to someone who is engaged in an expedition (for purposes of raiding, trade or exploration), and once he returns home a man is no longer a Viking but a Dane, Swede, Norwegian, Icelander or other native of whatever his homeland may be. That said, there was a distinct Viking Era (AD 793–1066), and the events of this time had major implications for European history.

Scandinavia was not greatly affected by the *Volkswanderung*. Its population gradually expanded, as did its wealth. During the Vendel Period (around AD 550–790), well-off Scandinavians imported horses from the Franks and were regarded as having herds second only to them.

The horse never played much part in Scandinavian warfare; even those who owned one would ride it to battle, then dismount to fight. The fairly dispersed population meant that most conflicts were fought between small war bands, and combat was thus a very personal matter. In this kind of fight, the sword was an excellent choice of weapon.

A fairly poor Scandinavian warrior might be armed with a spear and shield, with a knife as a backup weapon. Richer men favoured the axe or sword as their hand weapon, and some might bring a bow to a fight and use it whenever the opportunity arose. The Scandinavians did not field units of archers; even when massed battles took place, the bow was used by whoever had one whenever it was appropriate. Likewise, some men threw spears when the opportunity presented itself.

Scandinavian tactics were generally based around individual prowess, though fighting formations were used at times. The 'boar's snout' (*svinfylking*) formation was a wedge of fighting men designed to smash through an enemy's shield wall and bring about a general melee, in which the Norsemen excelled.

Few Norsemen were professional warriors. Most were farmers or traders (often a bit of both) who would fight when needed. Combat skills were passed on by those who had been successful in battle, and there were standard combat techniques that could be considered to form a basic 'Norse fighting system'. These included shield bashes and binds, hooking an enemy's shield with an axe, various sword blows and – if Icelandic sagas are to be believed – a defence against spears which was accomplished by jumping on to an enemy's spear with both feet to break it.

Some Norsemen carried the seax as a backup weapon. This was a large knife, much bigger and more effective in a fight than the working knife that most people carried. The seax was a true fighting-knife or perhaps a very small sword, and was actually preferred as a hand weapon by some warriors who favoured fighting at close quarters. Similar not-quite-sword weapons, such as the messer, have appeared at other times in history.

Thus the fighting forces of the Norsemen were warriors, not soldiers, and they fought as individuals. The sword, axe and seax were ideal weapons for this style of warfare, and were equally handy aboard ships and on the ground. This was probably not coincidence; even before the 'Viking Era', Norsemen made extensive use of ships for coastal and river trade, and for raiding their enemies.

The development of more seaworthy ships enabled longer expeditions, and permitted the Viking Era to begin. An expedition was defined to a Norseman as a trip in which it was necessary to work the oars in shifts. On a short voyage (i.e. a couple of hours or less) it was possible just to row to the destination, but an expedition required men to take turns at the oars. A 'Viking' was one who was engaged on such an expedition.

The Vikings were not merely bloodthirsty raiders. They usually owned farmsteads, and only joined an expedition when it seemed likely to be more profitable than running a farm or working at a craft such as blacksmithing. An expedition might be undertaken to explore an area, seeking new opportunities in the future or a place to settle as populations increased, but more commonly it was undertaken for profit.

Profit could be obtained by plundering or trade, and the Vikings were entirely happy to switch between the two when there was more profit to be made. Indeed, later in the Viking Era, there was a great deal of profit to be made by agreeing not to raid an area (in return for a large fee of course). This bribe was termed Danegeld, and permitted the Vikings to make money from one area by not raiding it, while raiding or trading elsewhere, or staying at home to work at their farms and crafts.

A raid might carry off plunder, but there were other ways to make money from raiding. Hostages were big business. Sometimes these were notable figures, such as Church officials, who could be held for an enormous ransom, but even humble farmers could be ransomed back to their families for a small profit. Sometimes this happened immediately after the raid was over, which was highly cost-effective as the hostage did not need transporting or feeding, and could get back to work generating wealth that could be targeted with a later raid.

Hostage taking, obviously, involved not killing the enemy. It was sometimes possible to round up captives at sword point, but some Viking raiders became skilled at disarming their opponents and forcing a surrender. Hostages were temporarily marshalled under guard near the Vikings' ships, with warriors sometimes returning several times with captives to add to the group. Those that could be ransomed were released; others were taken away to be sold as slaves.

The Vikings, then, were businessmen rather than destroyers. Some undoubtedly raided for the fun of it, and feuds could be very bloody. For the most part, however, an expedition was about profit, and there were no hard-and-fast rules about how that profit was to be obtained. The common denominator was usually the Viking longship, which was equally useful as a merchant transport and a raiding or combat vessel.

The Viking raiders achieved notoriety by attacking monasteries, which were usually located in remote areas far from help and filled with wealth. Although often depicted as pagans making war on God, in fact the Viking raiders were motivated by more earthly concerns, i.e. wealth and earning what they called word-fame for their deeds in battle.

Viking Armies

The Viking Era saw the raids increase from single ships or a handful of vessels to massive invasions involving hundreds of boats. The Norsemen also settled, sometimes in the places they had previously raided. They set up new homelands in the Shetland Isles, Iceland and Greenland, and even created a short-lived colony in Newfoundland.

Here, the Norsemen met the local people, who were still using Stone Age tools. Contemptuously calling them *skraelings* ('wretches'), the settlers cheated them in trade, and became their enemies. Although fortified and defended by men armed with the best European weapons technology, the Newfoundland colony was doomed from this point and had to be abandoned.

Other Norse groups pushed into what is now Russia, and became the military elite of a mixed Norse/Slavic society usually called the Rus. With centres in great cities such as Kiev and Novgorod, the Rus gradually evolved into what would become the early Russian kingdoms. In the interim, Norse traders used the rivers of Russia and Europe to trade with far-off places such as Baghdad and Constantinople. Norse traders pushed some distance up the Silk Road towards China, and encountered the advanced societies of the emerging Muslim states.

The Norsemen also came to the attention of the Byzantine Empire (formerly the Eastern Roman Empire), and many entered service with Byzantium as mercenaries. So many young men went off to seek work in Byzantium and the surrounding area that laws were passed among the Kievan Rus to prevent a man inheriting unless he came home and stayed.

Most famous among the Norsemen in Byzantine service were the Varangian Guard, who were notable for their use of two-handed axes as a primary weapon. The sword was carried as a sidearm and used in situations where swinging a two-handed axe might be counterproductive.

The Varangians were a disciplined military force, and were considered one of the finest fighting units of the ancient world. Former members, of course, took their skills home to the lands of the Rus or other parts of the Norse-influenced world from where they were recruited, and these lessons would not be forgotten. Experience gained in fighting the wars of Byzantium filtered through the Rus to their cousins in Scandinavia, who by the mid-800s were quite capable of fielding large armies and deploying them in distant campaigns using sea power.

By the middle of the 800s, the Vikings had moved from launching small raiding parties to sending large armies to plunder an area, and had settled in some regions. In Ireland, for example, Viking settlers became embroiled in the endless conflicts of the local population, and were soon just another faction rather than being foreign raiders.

In AD 865, a Viking army (which became known as the Great Heathen Army) invaded Britain via East Anglia, and began overrunning local kingdoms. Vikings gained control of Northumbria, East Anglia and Mercia, but were unable to defeat the Kingdom of Wessex under the command of Alfred the Great. This was not random destruction and pillaging (though a great deal of pillaging did occur); it was organised warfare between early English kingdoms and a coalition of Viking states. Nor was the nature of the fighting all that primitive.

The Military Art in the 'Dark Ages'

Some commentators still perpetuate the idea that for centuries after the fall of Rome, the military art collapsed into a dismal state. According to this view, warfare was a matter of individual warriors whirling crude and semi-blunt iron implements around their heads until they more or less accidentally killed someone. Despite the fact that it makes no sense, this view is still widely accepted.

While armies did as a rule become less uniformly equipped and trained, and organisational concepts such as proper logistics went rapidly downhill, the basic notions of tactics and skill at arms remained every bit as important. Indeed, since warfare was generally on a smaller scale after the fall of Rome, the individual warrior, fighting as part of a war band rather than an army, was more influential on the battlefield than before.

Most of those who engaged in military service did so only for a short time before returning to their homes, so complex training was not possible. However, basic battlefield manoeuvres were well understood, and skill at arms was often taught on an informal basis. A man might be shown how to handle his spear or axe by an uncle, a friend of his father, or a well-respected veteran of previous conflicts. Most of those who went into action as part of, or against, the Great Heathen Army had a working knowledge of how to use their weapons, and many had received good instruction from experts.

Alfred the Great was able to counter the strengths of the Viking force by a variety of measures. He constructed the first real navy that had ever existed in Britain, consisting of heavy vessels unsuited to open-water voyages but superior in defensive combat to the Viking longships. Fast-moving raiding parties were slowed by the creation of defended burghs, with fortifications that could be used as a base for a response force. Most importantly, he defeated the Viking army in the field and imposed a treaty on its leaders.

This treaty essentially divided England up between the Viking-controlled areas and the Anglo-Saxon regions. It also required the Viking leaders to be baptised as Christians, creating a new layer of complexity in the relations between European kingdoms.

Elements of the Great Heathen Army moved to the Continent to try their luck against the Frankish city of Paris. The city had already been sacked by Vikings several times. Viking fleets had become adept at using the rivers of France to penetrate deep inland before launching an attack. From pillaging villages and monasteries, the Vikings had progressed to plundering large cities or extorting tribute from them in what amounted to a continent-wide protection racket.

In 885, the Vikings attacked Paris again, besieging the city despite defensive measures such as fortifying bridges against them. Their fleet probably numbered around 300 ships, containing thousands of fighting men, though the claims by some contemporary chroniclers that they fielded 30,000–40,000 men are almost certainly exaggerated to an enormous degree.

Despite their numbers and the use of siege engines, the Vikings could not fight their way into Paris this time, and agreed to accept a bribe to continue upriver and attack Burgundy. This was an astute move on the part of the Frankish king, since Burgundy was in revolt at that time.

Paying one enemy to fight another seemed like a workable idea, but King Charles III of West Francia went one better. He granted lands along the coast to a large force of Vikings, and named their leader, Rollo, Duke of Normandy. At a stroke, Charles had changed the political situation entirely. Now his northern frontier was defended by the very men who had been pillaging it – future raids would fall upon them, and it was their swords that defended Francia from Viking incursions.

Norman Warriors

The Duchy of Normandy was established in AD 911, beginning a process that would meld the early Frankish feudal system with the looser and more energetic politics of the Vikings. Norman warriors became highly sought after as mercenaries as word of their fighting prowess spread. Fighting on foot or horseback, with a spear, sword and distinctive kite-shaped shield, the Norman warrior class evolved into a nobility of the sword as the feudal system took hold.

The mail-armoured warriors that made up the elite of the Norman armies were career soldiers, born to a life of training and warfare as a result of their parentage. Where their Viking ancestors were part-time raiders, traders and homesteaders, the Normans had a distinct noble class whose duties included administration and combat. This represented the beginning a new era in Europe, an age of kings and nobles, in which the primary combat asset was the armoured cavalryman.

The new system met the old at Hastings in AD 1066. Disputes over the English crown resulted in a three-way conflict between Harold Godwinson, who had been crowned king of England, Northumbrian rebels aided by King Harald Hardrada of Norway, and Duke William of Normandy. All three factions had candidates with valid claims to the English throne.

An army of Norsemen landed in Northumbria and defeated local forces that opposed them, but were then defeated in turn by Harold Godwinson's army at the Battle of Stamford Bridge. This clash was between two forces that fought in similar style. Most men were on foot, and the primary style of combat was that of the Viking or Anglo-Saxon warrior.

Marching south to contain Duke William's invasion from the Continent, Harold's force met the more organised army of the Normans. The Anglo-Saxon host was primarily composed of men who had a duty to serve a short time each year, and who were armed with simple equipment. This was sufficient against a similar force, but the combined-arms tactics of the Normans were a different matter.

Nevertheless, the Anglo-Saxon shield wall was able to repel repeated attacks, interspersed with barrages delivered by a corps of professional archers. The Norman infantry and cavalry both used the spear as their primary combat weapon, with the sword as a backup. These weapons were met by the two-handed axes of Anglo-Saxon housecarls (household infantry serving the nobility) and the spears of the common soldiery.

What happened at Hastings – William tempting the Anglo-Saxon force out of their defensive shield wall by a feigned retreat – is often described as a master stroke, but in fact it is far more likely that the Norman cavalry began to rout for real. Either way, the Anglo-Saxons began to pursue and were struck by a cavalry charge. Out of their defensive formation, the infantry were very vulnerable and suffered heavy casualties. Even this was not enough to break Harold's army, which re-established its defensive formation and fought on.

Finally, William attacked with his infantry and cavalry interspersed, and coordinated the charge with an overhead archery volley that dropped arrows into the Anglo-Saxons' rear ranks. This combined onslaught was too much for the Anglo-Saxons to withstand, and a party of Norman cavalry penetrated their line and reached King Harold.

Although Harold is depicted on the Bayeux Tapestry as taking an arrow in the eye, he was in fact killed by sword blows. These were delivered by armoured horsemen fighting as part of an organised feudal army, and they very graphically brought the Viking Age to an end. The same swords (more or less) served on both sides, but the way they were used, and the social system that wielded them, had changed. The age of the warrior was over, and the age of the knight was about to begin.

Creating the Warrior's Sword

European swords of the Migration Period (approximately AD 400–700) generally show similar characteristics to or direct influences from the Roman spatha. By the middle of the Viking Era, sword design had evolved a little, and a standard type was common in most areas.

The 'Viking sword', which saw use from Byzantium to Newfoundland, was a single-handed weapon with two cutting edges and a fairly rounded tip. Although not intended for thrusting, these swords could deliver an impaling stroke if the user tried hard enough. More than one saga hero is noted as having run his opponent through rather than cutting him.

Hand protection was fairly minimal, though a disc or, more commonly, a small, curved crosspiece was used. The definitive cruciform sword of the medieval period had not yet arrived, though the Viking sword was closely similar in many ways.

The blade was typically 70–80 cm long, with some shorter examples being made. Blades as long as 1 m have been discovered, but these are rare, and appeared late in the Viking Era. To reduce the weight of the weapon overall, the blade tapered towards the tip. This also had the effect of moving the point of balance rearwards, making the weapon more controllable. A heavy pommel counterbalanced the blade for the same reason.

Some examples of single-edged swords have been found, as widely separated as Ireland and Norway. Rather than being a different style of weapon, it is likely that these were cruder implements made either by an unskilled smith or by one who had to use inferior iron. The single-edged design allowed a wider back to the blade and therefore obtained greater strength from the same materials.

Video games and movies have given many people the impression that warriors' swords were extremely long, wide and heavy. The fact is that even the manliest Viking warrior could not fight using something resembling an ironing board with a broom handle sticking out of one end. Swords were typically 1–1.5 kg in weight, with 2 kg as the approximate upper limit.

This amount of weight offered a reasonable compromise between impact and controllability. A weapon that was too heavy would take too long to get moving and thus not be able to strike when the opportunity presented itself. It might deliver a massive impact, but it would be hard to recover for another stroke, leaving the user fatally vulnerable.

Ancient swordsmiths knew this, and made weapons that were effective in the hands of their intended user. Considerable variation in length can be encountered with warriors' swords; this is sometimes down to local preferences but could also be influenced by metallurgy. A long blade is subject to much greater stresses in combat, so it requires higher-quality steel and better swordsmithing if it is to survive a combat.

The standard way to create long blades in the Migration and Viking ages was to use pattern-welding. The raw materials took the form of iron bars, each with slightly different properties. Those with little carbon content created relatively soft iron, which remained flexible when formed into a blade. High-carbon bars created hard steel, which took and retained a good edge.

A stack of iron bars was heated and then drawn out into a long bar, which was twisted and hammered together with other composite bars. This was hammered out into the shape of the blade, creating a composite material of great strength and flexibility. It also created a distinctive patterning in the steel.

To ensure that they took a good edge, most blades were then given strips of hard steel on the cutting edges, which were then sharpened. Such blades generally took and held their edge better than those that were not so treated, but all the same there are numerous cases in Viking sagas of blades that became blunt in combat, and even of men stamping on bent swords to straighten them.

If a sword lost its edge, the mass of the weapon would still deliver a powerful blow, enabling the warrior to bludgeon his enemy to death.

This may be one source of the myth that all 'Dark Age' swords were blunt pieces of heavy, soft iron wielded by aggressive but unskilled clods.

The reality, however, is that the typical warrior's sword was a well-made and effective weapon – if it were not, he would have armed himself with something more useful! Weapons did become blunt in protracted combat, and would also have needed maintenance to remove nicks and notches from the blade. A nick represented a dangerous weak point, which could cause a sword to snap at a less than opportune moment. According to some of the Norse sagas, professional sword-sharpeners existed. This suggests that weapon maintenance was a profitable business.

Broken blades could sometimes be reforged into useful weapons. Examples have been found ranging from very good repair jobs to Frankenstein-like efforts that do not seem straight enough to be useful in combat, and were probably not trustworthy. Other blades could be salvaged by turning the remains into a knife or a spear point.

Towards the end of the Viking Era, the standard of metallurgy across Europe had improved to the point where it was no longer necessary to pattern-weld blades. The practice continued in some areas, but there was a general move towards homogenous steel blades. At the same time, the warrior's sword was evolving into the weapon used by feudal and medieval knights, and additional types were emerging.

The Norse Duel

The Norsemen used two forms of duel to settle differences between individuals. The original form was called Einvigi, and was in no way unique. Similar duels are recorded in England and the Germanic regions of Europe before the Viking Age. However, in many other regions the duel took on a religious or legal nature, and developed into the 'wager of battle' or 'trial by combat' that we shall discuss in the next chapter. To the Vikings, an Einvigi was nothing more than an agreed single combat between two individuals, with no spiritual overtones.

An Einvigi duel was a rather informal affair. It could be conducted anywhere and had no judges, no real rules, and did not establish who was right or wrong. Basically, two men agreed to fight because they had a dispute or because they hated one another, and all that mattered was who won. Although many would call upon the gods to help them in their fight, the Einvigi was all about the strength and prowess of the fighters. The winner got the credit, not his gods.

The idea behind the Einvigi custom was to act as a safety valve for tensions that might otherwise escalate into a blood feud, claiming many lives in raid and counter-raid with all of the associated economic and social disruption. However, many duels led to further ones, as relatives sought retribution for someone killed in the fight.

An Einvigi did not have to be 'fair'. A man who had armour could use it even if his opponent had none, and there were no rules about conduct. There was also no legal protection for someone who killed an opponent. Relatives of the deceased could still seek legal redress or pursue blood vengeance. In short, the Einvigi was nothing more than a custom of arranging to fight one to one rather than engaging in impromptu armed brawls that might involve several people at once.

In an effort to reduce the number of deaths in duels, and the ongoing feuds that often resulted, the Holmgang duel was created. This was a rather more formal affair, though it was still basically an agreed combat between men for the sake of honour. There were few legal implications, though failing to appear at the appointed time was a grave disgrace. The combatants could agree between themselves what the outcome would be, and this was considered binding. So a duel could be fought to force the opponent to admit he was in the wrong on some matter, or to pay a financial settlement. In the latter case, if the challenger was killed, his possessions were forfeit to the winner.

In a Holmgang duel, each fighter was armed with a sword, which was usually lighter than the usual war sword, and a rather flimsy shield. A second sword could be carried, usually on a thong looped around the wrist. Each fighter also had a shield-bearer, who carried two spare shields and could defend himself or 'his' fighter with them.

The shield-bearer would pass a new shield over when the duellist's own was splintered, and once he ran out of shields he had to withdraw from the fight. He was not permitted to attack the opponent (though he could issue his own challenge afterwards), so had no further role once his shields were gone. Once the duellist lost his last shield, he could only defend with his weapon (or weapons, if he had brought a spare).

Leaving the duelling area, which was normally marked by placing cloaks on the ground, was a loss, and carried with it connotations of cowardice. Retreating a step or placing one foot outside the duelling area attracted derision from onlookers – Norsemen were expected to stand their ground and fight!

The Holmgang duel was considered over when the first blood dripped on to the cloaks, and whoever had caused the bleeding was declared the winner. Fatalities were uncommon, as it was very difficult to deliver a single killing stroke, and in any case a death in a properly declared Holmgang was not considered grounds for blood vengeance. Likewise, the matter that had caused the Holmgang was considered settled, though a new quarrel about something else was not out of the question.

The Holmgang was intended to reduce the amount of blood feuding and vengeance-raiding going on at any given time. However, it was abused by some, who made their living by issuing frivolous challenges and demanding a settlement in cash or goods from the loser. Although perhaps despised, these professional duellists were acting legally and could not be outlawed even if their challenges were blatantly contrived.

The Holmgang duel seems to have acquired religious overtones as time went on, possibly because the customary duelling sites were often associated with holy places. Rituals were conducted at times to prevent evil magic from blunting the weapons of a duellist, and later in the Viking Era it seems that this became a standard part of preparing for a duel. However, the Holmgang was never a 'trial before God(s)' or anything similar – it was a fight between men, usually over very earthly matters, and the outcome was due to skill and strength rather than any idea of divine judgement.

It is interesting to note that while an Einvigi duel was basically an anything-goes scrap, honourable conduct was expected in the Holmgang. Biting, scratching, kicking and the like were not considered honourable but were fair play in the Einvigi. This move towards a 'fair fight' was probably for social reasons – the more fair and honourable the encounter was seen to be, the more likely its outcome was to be accepted.

By reducing the outrage and resentment caused by a lost fight, Viking society attempted to reduce the number of feuds or additional duels that followed on from an encounter. By and large, it worked fairly well. This is not an isolated concept; other duelling systems took a similar approach. Presumably the intent was that if violence could not be prevented, it should at least be regulated so that it was less likely to create more conflict.

Fighting with the Warrior's Sword

The swords of the 'warrior age' were, as already noted, typically long cutting weapons. Shields tended to be round, though later a family of kite-shaped shields, which combined a broad upper section to protect the body with a tapering lower area offering a horseman good defensive cover for his leg, was developed.

It is appropriate to consider the sword and shield as a single weapon system, with one of its components held in each hand. However, the sword could be used on its own. In this case, a warrior could best protect himself with a combination of movement and well-timed aggression. The warrior's sword was capable of parrying, and in some cases (such as a Holmgang) it might be the only means of defence available, but the warriors of Europe's so-called dark ages were not fencers.

Two-handed weapons were commonly used in this era. Spears might be used in one or two hands, and the large axes that were the main battlefield weapon of the Varangian Guard and many other forces had to be used in both hands. A warrior would carry his shield on his back while fighting in this manner, which gave him some protection from that quarter if someone got behind him. The shield would be brought round when the warrior switched to his sword or seax – perhaps because his axe was stuck in someone – or if the enemy began shooting arrows at him.

Two-handed swords were not used, and although there are claims that Vikings used their swords in both hands, this is problematical given the design of the hilt. There is simply no room for the other hand, other than a clumsy one-on-top-of-the-other grip. It is possible that a warrior who had lost his shield might strike a two-handed blow, however. This was accomplished by gripping the wrist of the sword hand with the left hand and using the added leverage to shove the strike through any defence.

Using the Shield

Under normal circumstances, the warrior armed with sword and shield used his shield both offensively and defensively. It could be passively held close to the body in the hope that a blow landed upon it. While not very scientific, this did provide a fair amount of defence for the warrior's body. Instinctively pushing out the face of the shield to block a blow was better, but still simplistic.

Blocking in this manner risked the shield being battered to pieces. Despite reinforcement around the rim and a covering of leather to reduce splitting, shields could quickly be hacked apart by a strong man armed with an axe or a good sword. A skilled shield user prevented this by not simply blocking square-on or passively using the shield as what amounted to a piece of armour. Instead, it was used for both attack and defence in a highly sophisticated manner.

The shield could be pushed forward to prevent the opponent from seeing exactly where the fighter's sword was or to conceal a stroke. It could also be driven forward to smother an attack, shoving the opponent's sword arm back rather than simply interposing the shield and allowing it to be hit. Since the weapon did not strike the shield, the shield would not be damaged.

Shoving with the shield could be used to pin the opponent's sword arm in what is termed a 'shield bind'. He was thus prevented from striking and was often made vulnerable to an attack around the edge of the shield. Before he could strike, the opponent had to free his sword arm, which could be prevented by relentless pressure. He might try to slip sideways off the bind, but a skilled warrior could feel what his opponent was doing though the shield, interpreting movements to predict his intentions, and manoeuvre to maintain the bind or deliver a killing stroke.

The shield could also be used to deliver a shield bash. This might take the form of a short, hard strike with the metal boss at the centre of the shield, or might be a headlong charge designed to send the opponent staggering or even knock him down. This was an effective, if somewhat risky, tactic in breaking up an enemy formation.

The raised shield would protect the warrior to at least some degree as he rushed forward and provided a hard striking surface to deliver the blow. However, this was a tactical movement rather than one intended to cause fight-ending injury. A downed or staggered opponent, or a formation that was penetrated, offered the warrior tactical advantages that could be followed up with the sword.

Defensively, the shield could be used to make a simple block, but a skilled user had more options at his disposal. By angling the shield correctly and moving close to the attacker, the defender could ensure that his opponent's arm, not his weapon, struck the shield. The curved surface and the central boss might hyperextend the opponent's arm, perhaps inflicting injury or causing a weapon to be dropped, but in any case the attack was nullified, with no damage to the shield. This also made it much more difficult to force a thrust over the shield.

The presence of the shield limited an enemy's options considerably. There was little point in bashing away at it, unless the intent was to hack it to pieces. This was a rather labour-intensive way of getting at an opponent, but it could work if the warrior had time to strike several blows. If the chaos of combat moved the opponents apart, all the effort expended upon the shield was wasted.

Since the shield covered much of the warrior's body, his opponent was normally restricted to striking at the head or perhaps the legs, though this could be risky. Knowing where attacks were likely aided the warrior in defence, as he could predict his opponent's actions. It also meant that a man who had a shield and a decent helmet was almost as well protected as his rich neighbour who had obtained a hauberk of mail.

Because the shield offered such an effective defence, it enabled even relatively unskilled fighters to adopt a defensive fighting style. As a rule, it is much easier to hit someone who has committed to an attack than an opponent who is ready to defend, but of course you first have to survive his attack. A shield-equipped fighter could afford to await an opportunity to strike a clean blow or to parry and counter, whereas a warrior who had less confidence in his defence might be better to go on the offensive and try to forestall the enemy's attack.

Ultimately, in order to win a fight, a warrior had to strike a blow, but the shield gave him a chance to pick his moment. It also facilitated that blow. An enemy who committed to an attack but struck the shield might leave himself open as his weapon recoiled. The shock of impact could disrupt his balance, preventing him from using his own shield effectively.

Alternatively, the shield could be used to conceal a counterblow or make it difficult for the attacker to parry. By raising his angled shield to block an overhead blow, the warrior hid everything below it from his opponent's sight. This facilitated a downward diagonal cut to the leg, under the opponent's shield. This counterstroke could be delivered as the enemy was still committed to the attack; raising the shield and beginning the counter-cut would be a single and well-practised action.

Using the Sword

The principal strokes with the long cutting sword are forehand diagonally down, more or less straight down, and backhand either diagonally down or horizontally. Upward forehand strokes are entirely possible when using a shield, but can lack power unless delivered correctly, and upward backhand strikes are not possible without raising the shield out of the way. This movement is made more difficult by the weight of the shield, and requires good coordination.

Thus the repertoire of the Viking, Frankish or Norman swordsman was seemingly limited. However, many variations of timing and combinations with the shield were possible. A swordsman who relied entirely upon hacking at his opponent would be less successful than one who knew how to work with sword and shield in conjunction. The very simplest of gambits, as already noted, was to await an attack, block it, and cut while the opponent was (hopefully) wide open.

A forehand diagonal stroke at the head or shoulder area could be countered by raising the shield and returning a forehand cut of the same type in a one-two action, but a more advanced fighter might instead take his sword arm across his body and cut diagonally upward with a backhand movement (his own shield is lifted out of the way by his parry) to strike the opponent under the arm. This took advantage of the opening and was impossible to parry with a shield held on the other side of the body.

An upward diagonal cut could be delivered under the shield, into the hip or upper leg area, or under the sword arm if the opponent had his hand well advanced. The same stroke could be used to knock a sword upward, perhaps creating an opening. Combinations of blows were far more likely to penetrate an opponent's defence than single attacks, though a swordsman who forgot about his own shield in his enthusiasm to keep attacking would likely receive a blow from a skilled opponent who knew how to balance attack and defence.

A combination of blows could be used to drive down the shield or to draw a response, then quickly land a cut elsewhere. This might not be a fight-ender, but any opportunity to wound an opponent and weaken him was a step towards eventual victory. Alternatively, a failed forehand cut (i.e. one that struck the shield) could be turned into a thrust by raising the elbow and pushing the tip forward. Even a fairly blunt-ended sword would cause serious injury if shoved into the opponent's face.

Normally the sword would be used in a manner that maximised the impact of the weapon, but it was equally possible to make an opportunistic cut near the tip of the blade or to lay the weapon's edge on the opponent's flesh and drag it to make it cut. Although not effective against armour, a cut of this sort could disable an opponent, and in any case it offered a chance to get something out of a situation where the swordsmen were in close contact and hard blows could not be struck.

More advanced swordsmen might use other tactics, such as feinting to draw a response with the shield then attacking elsewhere, or psychological gambits like a huge flat hack at the face, which might startle and alarm the opponent into an overcommitted defensive response. An opponent who could be induced to raise his shield in front of his face could not see what was coming next.

The key to much of this technique was to make use of the weight of sword and shield to counterbalance one another, and to use body mechanics to convert the energy from one strike into a response or follow-up. Keeping the sword and shield moving also helped deceive the opponent, who could not know whether a given movement was a fully committed attack.

Much use was also made of footwork. Standing still and bashing at one another was not very productive, so outside the Holmgang duel a fighter would make use of his mobility. If he could draw his opponent into a committed attack then move just slightly out of reach, he would gain an excellent opportunity for a counterstroke. Generally speaking, fighters would open and close the range, and would tend to circle one another.

Moving towards the opponent's sword was a poor idea under most circumstances, so fighters would tend to circle to the right. This would place their shield in front of the opponent's weapon but open up a line of attack for their own weapon. Of course the opponent would likely match the movement, so a fight between two individuals would tend to revolve anticlockwise most of the time.

What a skilled fighter would not do was waste energy on large, committed blows without any real chance of success. Not only was this a rapid route to exhaustion but it left him open to a counter-attack. He would keep his weapon positioned to threaten the opponent, and would be always mindful of the adage that 'many a man who is slain shall avenge himself'. In other words, warriors were well aware that few sword blows would instantly kill or incapacitate their opponents.

There was no point in making an attack that left the warrior open. Reaching far under the shield to cut at the ankle might seem clever, but a fighter who did so would almost certainly be hit in the head or the back even if he struck his blow first. Similarly, an opponent who received a death-blow might still be able to make a few more cuts, and might well be recklessly determined to take his slayer with him. The swordsman who paused to admire his fight-winning stroke might be killed by his dying opponent.

Thus it was necessary to fight with caution, and a skilled warrior would do so. Reckless fools who rushed in flailing would not last long, whereas the warrior who picked his moment or drew an enemy into doing what he wanted then countered, and who made good use of movement to get in for an attack and out again afterwards, would live much longer. He was likely to survive to pass on his skills to others, ensuring that the art of the warrior survived into future generations of swordsmen.

CHAPTER 4

Blades of Chivalry: The Medieval Longsword

The Medieval Period, or Middle Ages, began with the fall of Rome in the fifth century AD, and came to an end in the fifteenth century with the Renaissance. The early part of this era, as we have seen, was characterised by the rise of what might be termed warrior kingdoms, which gradually evolved into the feudal societies of the High Middle Ages. This is considered to have begun around AD 1000, and continued until the Renaissance took hold, though this point varies from one part of Europe to another.

The transition was of course gradual, and was a combination of several factors. Climate change led to a warm period in which crops flourished. This abundance of food led to population growth, which helped drive some social changes. At the same time Christianity was spreading across Europe and technology was advancing.

During this time, the armoured horseman had come to dominate European battlefields. Protected by mail armour and armed with lance, shield and sword, this heavy cavalryman represented a powerful concentration of military force in a small number of men. This was socially desirable to the feudal societies of the time, enabling a warrior elite to rule and dominate their less well-armed subjects.

The Middle Ages saw the rise of the armoured knight, whose code of chivalry has been the subject of many stories. Yet the term 'chivalry' did not originally refer to any particular virtue – the word comes from the French *chevalier*, referring to someone who owned a horse. A similar term for a nobleman is the German *Ritter*, meaning 'rider'.

The ability to purchase and maintain a suitable mount was an indication of wealth and power, and of course at that time wealth and power were in the hands of the military class. But being a horse-owner did not imply any more than this; the idea of courteous knights bound by a code of chivalry was some way in the future.

So was the 'shining armour' commonly associated with medieval knights. In AD 1000 a long coat of mail, heavy boots and an open-faced helm with a nasal bar represented standard equipment for the heavy cavalryman. This offered very good protection from most of the weapons available at the time, but was not really much better than the armour available to richer Gallic or Norse warriors of the preceding few centuries.

The mail coat was generally worn over a gambeson, or padded jacket, created by quilting thick cloth and stuffing it with resilient material such as horsehair. A gambeson was reasonably effective against many weapons when worn alone, and when combined with a mail coat it offered excellent protection. The mail spread out an impact and prevented cutting or piercing weapons from penetrating, while the padding underneath helped absorb impact.

Mail was extremely hard to penetrate with the weapons of the day, even when not backed by padding. Remains have been found dating from the early Middle Ages with marks on leg bones in the shape of mail rings. This indicates that the wearer survived an impact that was hard enough to impress his armour onto his thigh bone through the flesh of his leg … and that he went on to live for a considerable period afterward.

Blunt instruments, or those that concentrated a lot of force at one point such as axes and heavy swords, could harm an armoured man through his mail. Impaling weapons such as spears were generally defeated by chainmail unless they struck home cleanly rather than skidding off, though some lighter forms of mail could be penetrated by very slim daggers, which were stiff enough to pop open the links.

Of course, a padded gambeson was hot to wear, especially in the exertion of a fight. Mail was not only heavy but also suffered from poor weight distribution. Most of the weight of armour fell on the shoulders and waist, where the mail was supported by a belt. This was not as much of a problem for a mounted man as for one fighting on foot, of course, but it did mean that armour was tiring even for those conditioned to its weight.

Mail did not offer complete invulnerability, but it did make a warrior very hard to kill. Combined with a helmet and shield, it offered few unprotected targets. A man who was too tired to move, or who had been downed, could be battered to death by heavy blows or stabbed through a vulnerable point, but one that retained his mobility had a huge advantage over an un-armoured opponent.

For the un-armoured man, any strike with a cutting or impaling weapon was certain to cause injury. Blunt instruments would harm him on even a glancing strike, but a marginal hit on a mailed warrior might have no effect whatsoever. He had another advantage, this one psychological. A man who knows he is well protected will be more confident than one who feels vulnerable, so a warrior feeling the comforting weight of his armour might be more willing to make a decisive attack – and more likely to survive if it were misjudged.

Terminology regarding mail armour varies from place to place, but as a general rule a thigh-length or shorter mail coat was referred to as a haubergon and a longer coat, often reaching to the knees, was a hauberk. The warriors of the Carolingian dynasty (in what is now France) wore an item known as a byrnie, which may have been a mail coat or mail rings sewn on to heavy leather backing.

Other items fashioned from chainmail became available as time went on. These included mailed gauntlets, a mail hood to protect the head (known as a coif), mailed leg protection in the form of trousers (chausses) and mail attached to a helmet to protect the neck (aventail or camail). The latter was not a new invention; some Norse warriors used a similar device composed of a mail neck and shoulder guard hanging from the helmet. In conjunction with a shield this offered protection almost as good as a mail shirt under most circumstances, and at a fraction of the cost.

The armoured horseman benefited from another development that was becoming prevalent at the time, the stirrup. Early stirrups were simply leather loops, and archaeologists are divided over exactly when these entered common use. Different designs have been found in several places, making a precise date of adoption difficult or even impossible to pinpoint. Stirrups may have been introduced into Europe by the successive waves of mounted barbarians arriving from the east in the years AD 500–800, gradually being adopted by European horsemen over time.

The stirrup itself was not enough to revolutionise warfare. It needed to be paired with a new design of saddle known as a treed saddle. This used a wooden frame to distribute the load; without the saddle tree, heavy use of stirrups would harm the mount. The combination of both facilitated an evolution in horsemanship that made mounted weapons use far more effective.

It has been suggested that the adoption of the stirrup allowed mounted men to charge with their lances couched (i.e. held under the arm) rather than stabbing with them to the sides as they passed the target, but again evidence is conflicting. It was possible to use the stirrups as an anchor, pushing forward and down with the legs to force the rider back against the rear of the saddle. This enabled the impact of a lance charge to be better withstood, but how much this altered the nature of warfare is questionable – there is evidence that some warriors used their lances in an underarm couched manner before the adoption of stirrups.

What is certain is that stirrups helped a rider remain on his horse in the chaos of a fight, allowing him to regain his balance after his mount had shied or if he had leaned too far while striking or avoiding a blow. He could also stand up in the stirrups to deliver an overhead cut with the sword, generating immense power with the assistance of gravity. Thus even if he were very tired the armoured horseman was still combat-effective, and so long as he stayed on his mount he had a good chance of survival. The stirrup was of enormous assistance in these areas.

The lance was the primary weapon of the armoured horseman, along with lighter spears that could be thrown. These weapons gave the mounted man good reach both in front of him and to the sides; he could ride past an opponent and spear him without approaching closely enough to be endangered by a shorter weapon. Stirrups allowed him to lean further and put more behind a blow, and to recover from mistakes more readily. However, at some point it was likely that the cavalryman would break or lose his lance, at which stage he resorted to his sidearm.

The Arming Sword

The armoured cavalryman normally carried a long, straight sword as a sidearm. Usually referred to as arming swords, these weapons were capable of cutting or thrusting, and were long enough to reach an opponent from the horse. This was extremely important; a cavalryman might have to fight against infantrymen who were clustering around him or to cut at a mounted opponent. His mount would be willing to approach only so close to the target; the rest of the distance had to be closed with metal.

There is a persistent myth that medieval weapons were huge, clumsy things of great weight, but this is simply not so. A weapon of this sort would be impossible to wield effectively and would be likely to get the user killed. Arming swords were in fact well made and often very finely balanced. A sword was the symbol of nobility as well as a fighting tool, and both purposes were served by owning a good one.

The arming sword was obviously intended for use 'in harness', i.e. when wearing armour, but was also carried when in civilian clothing. In many societies a gentleman was not properly dressed if not equipped with his sword, a custom that survived in some cultures until very recent times, though in many cases it became acceptable to replace the sword with a dress dagger.

The arming sword evolved from earlier 'warriors' swords', as discussed in the previous chapter, though it gained a broader hand guard with very pronounced quillions. These helped protect the sword arm, notably from an opponent's cut that skipped from the blade and could then land on the sword arm. This was a significant threat when fighting on horseback, though armour would normally nullify it unless the wearer was very unlucky. Quillions did offer some protection but they were not primarily defensive in nature. Instead, they were used to bind an opponent's blade.

As the opponent's blade slid along a swordsman's weapon towards his hand, he could turn his blade, and angle the weapon as a whole so that the opponent's blade became trapped between the quillions and the strong part of the swordsman's own blade. This movement was used to disarm an opponent, and could in theory break a sword. More commonly, it enabled a swordsman to gain control of the opponent's blade, preventing him from following up an attack while the swordsman prepared his counter stroke.

The arming sword was not a 'fencing' weapon as such; it was primarily a battlefield sword that would normally be used with a shield. However, a nobleman forced to fight out of armour could use his weapon to both attack and defend. He was trained to grapple and grasp the opponent with his empty shield hand. His fighting style would make use of mobility and timing for defence, in preference to parries with the weapon, and he might well defend by cutting into the attack rather than making a parry and riposte, but the option was available.

This was of course because the arming sword was not a clumsy hacking tool. It had the mass to pose at least some threat to an armoured opponent, but it was light enough to be used with subtlety and skill. During the tenth to twelfth centuries, the blade was typically about 75–80 cm long, and although designs varied somewhat this weapon was fairly standard in most areas. Arming swords generally acquired a pronounced taper from the hilt to the tip, retaining their cutting capabilities but at the same time enabling a thrust to penetrate heavier armour.

From the twelfth century onward, arming swords began to evolve, and two distinct families emerged. This was a result of advances in armour design; the existing weapon was insufficient to reliably inflict injury through armour. One family of arming swords gained a longer and heavier blade for the purpose of increasing the impact of the weapon. The other was shorter, very stiff, and had a very effective point for the purpose of punching through armour.

These two weapon designs resulted in a divergence in fighting styles to some extent. The heavy cutting blade could still be used in much the same manner as its lighter predecessor, but cuts had to be launched from a solid base and driven home with great force. Likewise, thrusts had to be driven in hard, which required significant setting-up of the attack if they were to be effective.

In both cases, an opponent who was able to move around could magnify the effectiveness of his armour by doing so. A thrust might glance off or reach the opponent as it became spent; likewise a heavy cut could be mitigated by moving away from it or into it. The latter shortened the arc of the cut and weakened it to the point where the impact might not be significant.

One answer to this problem was to grab and grapple the opponent, ideally causing him to fall. A man on the ground, or one backed up against a solid object and thus unable to evade or mitigate the attack by movement, was much easier to kill than one who was able to fight back effectively.

The arming sword remained the standard sidearm for noblemen and armoured cavalry throughout the medieval period, but became increasingly ineffective against heavily armoured opponents as time went on. It was better than nothing of course, and was entirely adequate against lesser-armoured opponents, but for the battlefield the one-handed sword was no longer a good choice of weapon. A variety of axes, maces, picks, flails and spears (or cut-down lances) became standard weapons for battling on horseback or on foot against other armoured opponents.

Among the weapons that emerged as effective against all comers was the two-handed sword. Known by various names, these weapons emerged in the early 1300s and were in widespread use until around 1550. After that, some cultures retained them, although their applications changed. The two-handed sword, or longsword, was employed in a different manner to the arming sword, and will be considered separately.

In general, fighting with an arming sword was not very different from using the warrior's sword discussed in the previous chapter. It was primarily a cutting tool intended for use with a shield, and was used in much the same manner as a Norseman's sword would have been in the preceding centuries. However, fighting styles did evolve as armour improved. Precise blows became more necessary in order to penetrate weak points, and techniques for setting these up were evolved.

When fighting without a shield, the sword was used for both attack and defence. Defence could also be accomplished by use of measure (distance). The most obvious way to accomplish this was to use mobility, staying out of range and then advancing rapidly to the attack, retiring if it failed and then trying again. However, this was both tiring and not always reliable; the opponent could also move and might follow a retirement or himself move out of reach.

A more subtle use of distance was to sway forward and back without moving the feet. Some opponents would of course charge in close, but most were mindful of the prospect of being hit and would fight from a predictable measure. Cuts were not made with the part of the blade close to the hilt, as this would not only require the swordsman to move very close to the opponent and thus expose him to counter-attack as he closed in but also would be less effective, as this part of the blade moves much more slowly than the tip.

Thus the most competent swordsmen would attempt to deliver a cut with a part of the sword that offered the best combination of reach and effectiveness, and this point was quite near the tip. A movement of just a few inches would suffice to move the swordsman's head and body out of reach of such a cut. Thus he could lean in a little to make his attack and sway back afterward, altering the distance between his opponent's sword and its target enough that it passed harmlessly by. By not moving his feet the swordsman remained close enough to make another attack by swaying forward again.

These movements were not hugely exaggerated, and had to be finely judged, but a properly trained swordsman could confound his opponent and then disable him without needing to move around or make anything resembling a parry. Conversely, the swordsman could close in and seize his opponent's sword arm or use a variety of trips and other wrestling movements to put him in a vulnerable position.

Formal parries, in the sense of placing the sword in the way of an attack as a purely defensive movement, and then launching a riposte after the attack was dealt with, were possible but were not ideal for this kind of combat. A fairly heavy blade, moving fast, would deliver a great deal of impact to the parrying weapon, which might cause damage and could well knock aside a parry. The alternative was to use the same cuts defensively as for offence, but to direct them into the attack rather than at the opponent.

Cutting into the attack had a number of advantages. Notably, it required the swordsman to learn a smaller body of technique, and used natural movements that aligned the weapon in its strongest manner – the sword was constructed to withstand the impact of striking armour in this alignment; hitting another sword was quite similar, whereas a formal parry imposed a different set of stresses.

Most importantly, cutting into the attack used the weapon's mass and movement to knock aside the incoming blow, making defence against heavy cuts more certain. The shock of receiving a cut on the blade is transmitted to the swordsman's arm and can be tiring; counter-attacking shares the impact out more evenly between both combatants.

If well timed, these counter-cuts did more than stop the attack. A combination of slight movement and an attack against the blade could deflect an incoming cut and send the attacker's weapon out of position, leaving him wide open for a strike to his head, body or sword arm. Some counter-cuts were 'stop cuts' directed at the attacker's arm. Whatever injury they caused, in order to be effective stop cuts they had to defeat the attack by striking the arm hard enough, or else the swordsman would be struck anyway.

The key to using a single fairly heavy weapon in attack and defence was to make use of its weight and momentum. If the blade was moving then it made more sense to keep it moving, using body mechanics to redirect it, rather than stop it and start it going in a different direction, which would require more effort. Time plays an increasingly important role in fighting with heavy swords, as they take longer to change direction or start moving than lighter weapons.

Sometimes the timing is such that there is simply no way to get to an attack in time or to hit an opponent who is wide open. This is most likely to occur if the swordsman takes wild or desperate swings. A tighter, more disciplined fighting style prevents most such errors. While the movements might be graphic and violent they were also highly skilled and well controlled, at least by swordsmen who wanted to survive to teach others.

If the blade was static, then a high guard position enabled the swordsman to take advantage of gravity when he wanted to start moving, although various positions were used. Most guard positions were not so much about where the blade was but what it could do from there; they created a threat space and implied consequences for the opponent if he took certain actions rather than making those actions impossible. The effect was the same in most cases – few warriors would charge in if they knew their attack could be easily knocked aside and countered.

Thus fighting with the arming sword combined use of effective ready positions and an assessment of the possibilities each offered with an instinctive understanding of the behaviour of the weapon when moving or in contact with another blade. A less skilled swordsman might just swing his weapon and hope for the best, but a properly trained warrior was much more in control of the weapon and the course of the fight. He knew what his opponent could do next, and what he could not, and was already moving to counter or evade when the attack was launched. His own attacks were well enough controlled that he did not compromise his defence.

This was not 'fencing' as such; it was battle on a personal scale. However, the principles that would later be enshrined in the various fencing systems already existed. Most importantly, the swordsman knew that he must hit without being hit, which might mean passing up an opportunity to attack if there was too much risk involved. Those who learned this lesson tended to live longer than those who just picked up a sword and swung it at an opponent's head.

Advances in Armour Technology

The construction of plate armour dates back at least to Ancient Greece, where some warriors were equipped with thick breastplates and greaves to protect the legs. Fashioned of bronze, these armour pieces were heavy and could only protect parts of the body that did not need to bend or flex very much. Plate armour fell into disfavour for many years, re-emerging in the thirteenth century and being developed through the fourteenth.

This new generation of plate armour was of good steel rather than heavy bronze, creating plates that could offer better protection for less weight. Armour could also be constructed from articulated groups of smaller plates rather than large single pieces, allowing freedom of movement without compromising protection.

Mail was still used of course. Early plate armour – the term 'plate mail' is not really correct, since mail implies rings rather than plates – was a combination of plate and chainmail over a padded backing. In essence, at first plate reinforced the chainmail by adding rigid protection at vulnerable points, but later the balance shifted and armour began to be made primarily of plates, with chainmail covering points that were difficult to armour in plate.

Armour did become quite heavy, particularly specialised tournament armour. This was heavier than standard battle harness, incorporating reinforced plates to make jousting safer, or additional components. An example of this is the tonlet, essentially an armoured skirt that gave additional protection to the upper legs. Armour of this sort can be considered sporting equipment rather than combat gear; it was simply too heavy for use in battle, but allowed the wearer to compete in a tournament in greater safety.

Battle armour had to be light enough to wear all day and to fight for hours if necessary. Being on a horse helped, and the improved weight distribution of plate rather than mail armour meant that armour did not feel as heavy – plate was more tiring than burdensome. While the armour was indeed weighty it did not restrict a properly conditioned man from doing anything he could do unencumbered. Far from needing a winch to lift them on to their horses as has been at times suggested, some knights would show off by vaulting into the saddle or performing handstands in their armour.

Armour could make it difficult to get up if the wearer were downed, and if it were buckled by heavy impacts it might restrict movement or breathing. However, most of the myths of overburdened knights tottering about are dispelled by historical evidence as well as common sense – a cavalryman who could not quickly mount a horse would not be a military asset, and one who could barely walk in his armour was not going to be able to fight effectively.

Heavy armour eventually fell into disuse, but again the popular idea of why is a myth. Armoured knights were not blasted from the battlefield by commoners armed with muskets. High-quality plate armour was quite capable of resisting a musketball; indeed, before it was accepted by the user a piece of armour was 'proven' by shooting it! Armour that did not have proof-marks from ball impacts would not be considered a worthwhile investment.

The decline of heavy armour stemmed from a number of social, economic and technological changes that took place towards the end of the medieval era rather than an inability to keep pace with weapons technology. Full plate was gradually replaced by partial or half-plate, and over time most kinds of armour faded from the battlefield.

Armour did not completely disappear, however. In the Napoleonic era there was a revival in body armour as some nations fielded cuirassiers, heavy cavalry equipped with breastplates (in some cases breast and back, in others chest only) and heavy helmets. Other cavalry wore just a helmet, often augmented by a rolled cloak worn diagonally across the left shoulder and chest. This offered some protection from a sabre cut, for which the left shoulder was a common target. Some hat designs offered good head protection without being, ostensibly at least, armour.

However, the need for heavy swords to counter plate armour declined at the same rate as the armour itself was abandoned. The two-handed sword remained in use for some other purposes, however, as we shall see.

Medieval Warfare

There is a common misconception that medieval warfare was a fairly clueless business, in which mobs of knights charged at one another seeking a suitable (i.e. socially equal or higher) opponent with whom to engage in a contest of honour, footsoldiers were treated with contempt, and strategy was non-existent. This perception has some basis in fact but it is a gross distortion of reality.

It is true that the armies of the medieval era could be undisciplined much of the time. This was largely a product of a culture in which a nobleman's worth was tied to his prowess at arms and his performance in battle. Accusations of cowardice, or even of hanging back a little, were ruinous, creating a climate in which there was a strong social impetus to get stuck in and be seen engaging before others. Some commanders were able to curb this tendency to some extent, but it was a fact of medieval life that the system which created potent armoured cavalrymen also turned them into a blunt projectile liable to launch itself in the general direction of the enemy at the first possible opportunity.

Despite this, medieval commanders had a keen grasp of the politico-economic reasons for war and the means by which it could be won. Rather than seeking to defeat the enemy in open battle and then trying to dictate a treaty, campaigns were generally directed at the capture of centres of power – typically castles and cities – or the destruction of enemy resources.

The capture of a castle or a fortified city was often a lengthy business, in which various types of specialist troops and footsoldiers in general played a part that was universally recognised as important. Credit always went to the knightly class, but the role of commoners under arms was not forgotten by a successful commander. Change of ownership of a strong place such as a major castle was not only an economic benefit to the captor but it showed the loser to be weak, damaging him politically and perhaps forcing him into negotiations.

Likewise, the tactic of raiding was used extensively. Various types of raid existed; there were technical terms for many of them, suggesting that this was a well-established and carefully studied part of warfare. All were intended to weaken the enemy politically and economically. Raiding not only destroyed the enemy's economy and gathered supplies for the raiders to use in further operations, but it also demonstrated the inability of the raided lord or king to protect his holdings.

Raids and sieges often resulted in field battles, but rather than these being the point of the campaign, they were generally fought to facilitate or prevent other, war-winning, actions. Thus, rather than the intent being to seek out the enemy, engage and defeat him, the medieval commander tended to focus more on obtaining political or economic advantages and fought only as necessary to do so.

Most forces that were fielded were built around the armoured knight as the main striking force, backed up by other troops of varying value. Some, like English longbowmen or Genoese crossbowmen, were highly skilled and were sometimes professional soldiers. Others were simply a levy of hastily raised troops equipped with basic weapons.

In between the nobility and the ill-armed peasantry there existed in most areas a middle class composed of professionals and specialists of various sorts. These included professional fighting men who were not noblemen. They were armed and equipped according to local fashion and what they could afford, ranging from light infantry, armed with a spear, shield, helmet and perhaps a gambeson, to what were essentially knights in all but name.

In any given body of what appeared to be armoured knights, some men might be commoners, professional soldiers of what was termed the 'serjeant' class. The best-off of these might be armed and armoured exactly like a knight of the same region, while others were more lightly equipped but still able to ride with the heavy cavalry and fill out numbers. All the members of the heavy cavalry force were collectively known as men-at-arms, but only some of them held noble rank and could thus correctly be called knights.

Knights proper were the social elite, men who held a title and a position in society as part of the military ruling class. Some among them were higher nobles – barons, counts and even princes – and command was by social rank rather than strategic competence. That said, members of the knightly class trained for war as part of their duties and were schooled in more academic aspects of war-making such as politics, strategy and siegecraft.

The usual formation for a medieval army was three 'battles', each containing a mix of troops. When battle was joined, these three battles swung from the line of march into a combat deployment, forming the centre plus left and right wings. In theory, each battle was self-contained, and would often fight against its opposite number in an engagement that might as well be separate from the actions of other battles.

Some commanders did use more sophisticated tactics, such as massed longbowmen, protected by dismounted knights and men-at-arms, positioned on a hill to weaken the enemy's charge. The combination of the fire of the archers or crossbowmen and the shock effect of the cavalry charge could crumble and then shatter an enemy force where each alone was unlikely to succeed, and many commanders made good use of this principle.

Once combat was joined, a knight or man-at-arms might find himself fighting on foot, although mounted combat was often considered preferable. His opponents might be armoured horsemen or footsoldiers, lighter-equipped infantry or cavalry, or he might find himself surrounded by a mob of determined but not very skilled peasants. In some campaigns he might be engaged by light cavalry or even horse archers.

Armed solely with hand weapons, the knight's only effective tactic was to get into close contact and fight it out. In the close action of a horsed or foot melee, individual fighting power was paramount. Good protection, which still left the user able to move freely, coupled with powerful weaponry and the skill to use it, would carry the day in many cases. This skill (and the physical conditioning to go with it) was developed in long training, and tested in the tournament.

Chivalry and the Tourney

As already noted, the term 'chivalry' originally referred to being the owner of a warhorse, and therefore a member of the upper social class. Over time, the expectations placed on such individuals gradually evolved into what is today recognised as the 'code of chivalry', which varied somewhat from place to place but essentially set forth the ideals of the knightly class.

The basic concepts of this code were fairly simple. Knights were expected to be courageous and loyal to their social superiors, forthright and honest, and upholders of the Church. Some aspects of this code were very beneficial to a knight in a tight spot – if forced to surrender, he could often go free after promising to pay a ransom, which was a useful form of life insurance. The society of the time was such that a knight's word could usually be trusted, as he would be socially ruined if he did not keep it.

Other aspects of the code of chivalry were somewhat hypocritical. The nobility were to respect the honour of women ... but this only really applied to noblewomen. Peasant girls could be treated as a knight wanted, if he were so inclined. Likewise, the degree of piety and selflessness suggested by the code of chivalry was in practice rarely met.

The reality of the chivalrous knight concept was that it varied from place to place and man to man. There really were paragons of the storybook knight in shining armour, who did good deeds out of devotion to God, King and Chivalry. Others were little more than armoured thugs with a title. However, there were some situations where even the most unpleasant of knights had to follow the rules or risk social ruin. One such occasion was the tournament.

Originally, the tourney was a rough and ready affair that amounted to little more than an agreement among several knights to meet up and have a fight. Tourneys were fought with live (sharp) weapons, and often resulted in death or disablement of good fighting men. The Church and many rulers tried to discourage the practice, but there were complications.

The tournament was an excellent way of producing extremely skilled warriors who were mentally prepared for the rigours of combat, so it was not necessarily desirable to forbid it. In any case, such an injunction would likely be ignored by men who wanted to prove themselves and whose emerging code of chivalry did not permit them to refuse a challenge from a social equal.

The answer was to create rules that limited the violence of the tourney while retaining its usefulness as a training environment. Thus were created a number of events that are today familiar to us, such as jousting in which the intent is to knock one another off the horse, or variants where the aim was simply to break a light lance on the opponent's shield. There was also the 'tourney proper', in which everyone charged into the combat area and laid about them. The last man remaining mounted was declared the winner. There were also foot combats, between matched and unmatched weapons, and melees involving several combatants.

Attitudes to the tourney varied. The English nobility generally considered a tournament to be a serious preparation for combat, which also had social connotations and made a grand spectacle. The French considered the event itself as highly important, with the training aspects coming second. Either way, a good performance not only helped a man maintain his reputation in a society that judged him on his ability to fight but it also spared him the pain of injuries taken while being defeated.

The tournament not only helped encourage individuals to stay in training during peacetime, it also served as a crucible to develop techniques of weapon handling. What worked against a determined foe in the tourney would presumably work on the battlefield. If there were flaws in the fighting system being taught to young men-at-arms, they were better identified early and modified, rather than being shown up in the heat of battle.

The trial by combat, or judicial duel, was distinct from the tourney but similar in some ways. Essentially, guilt or innocence, or who had the right of a dispute, was determined by a fight to the death or disablement. A fighter could surrender, but was outlawed in addition to being proven guilty or wrong. For a nobleman this was unthinkable.

For commoners, there were various rules and customs regarding the judicial duel, some of them quite bizarre. For a dispute between knights, the situation was more like a very small tourney. Conventions would be agreed regarding choice of weapons and style of combat, and the fight itself conducted in front of an audience of nobles and possibly commoners as a major social event. In some cases, the sword would be the chosen weapon for the duel. Even if it were not, it would be carried as a backup in case the main weapon were lost or damaged.

The Longsword

The two-handed sword has been given many names, both during its time in service and by later historians. Often referred to as the longsword, these weapons are also sometimes called great swords and a variety of other names, of which many refer to a specific type. We shall reserve the term 'great sword' for the very large two-handed weapons that emerged at the end of the Middle Ages, in order to preserve the distinction between the medieval weapon and its larger Renaissance counterpart.

The medieval longsword was not as long as its name might imply. Blades were typically 90–110 cm in length, and in many cases much the same as a one-handed sword. The longer handgrip gave the weapon a greater overall length of course, but the longsword did not have significantly greater reach than an arming sword. Nor was it much heavier.

The impression that medieval swords were hugely oversized comes mainly from video games and other inaccurate depictions; it is simply not possible to fight with a blade that is wider than a man's body. The longsword offered a good balance between having enough weight to strike hard and being sufficiently light to move quickly.

The longsword initially had a simple form, with a crosspiece to protect the hands and to trap the opponent's blade. Evolution did take place, but the highly complex two-handed swords of the Renaissance did not appear overnight. The fairly simple longsword served its users well enough that it retained its form throughout the period of 1350 to 1550 or so, and examples remained in use alongside more complex later designs.

The bastard sword, or hand-and-a-half sword, falls somewhere in between the realms of one-handed and two-handed weapons. Designs varied, but for the most part a bastard sword had the same blade length as a typical arming sword of the era, with a tapering blade suitable for thrusting or cutting. The weapon had an elongated handgrip, allowing it to be used in one or both hands.

If used in one hand, the bastard sword functioned much like an arming sword, though its balance would be slightly different. Two-handed use permitted heavier strokes to be delivered, which could defeat heavy armour or sever the limbs of less well-protected opponents. A sword used in both hands was also effective against the legs of horses.

One major driving factor in the adoption of the two-handed sword was armour. The need for a more powerful weapon to defeat heavy armour was coupled with the improved protection of that very armour, which meant that a warrior did not necessarily require a shield. The greater reach and hitting power of his weapon gave him numerous advantages in combat, but of course he had also to use his sword for defence.

The use of a longsword required a new body of technique, and various systems developed to make use of the weapon's unique characteristics. Normally, the weapon was used with both hands on the grip. The primary hand (the one that would hold a one-handed sword, almost always the right) was closest to the crosspiece, with the secondary hand closer to the pommel, to provide leverage.

This grip allowed the longsword to be used with great subtlety when required. The weapon could be swung from the shoulders to create a powerful stroke, or could be manipulated without much arm movement. This allowed the blade to change direction or alignment in a small space, which might deceive the opponent about the swordsman's intentions. Heavy collisions between blades could be better soaked up by a two-handed grip.

The weapon could also be used with one hand just in front of the crosspiece, or quite a long way down the blade. Known as half-swording, this technique supported the leading part of the blade and could be used to drive a thrust home with both power and precision. In some systems the weapon could be held entirely by the blade and the pommel or crosspiece used to strike with, or the quillions might be used to hook and trip an opponent.

Conventionally held with both hands on the hilt, the longsword did not require a great deal of space to use but could still deliver powerful, armour-defeating blows. As with the arming sword, techniques for its use combined effective ready positions with an understanding of how the weapon behaved in movement. Many longsword techniques were based around its ability to change direction abruptly. For example, a cut that met the opponent's blade could be turned into a thrust and levered past the defence. This could also be done with a one-handed weapon but the use of both hands greatly facilitated this kind of action.

The guard postures used with the longsword may, in some cases, seem fanciful to the observer. They were based on what the weapon could do from that position, as with the arming sword. Thus a swordsman who appears to the uninformed observer to be wide open may in fact be quite well defended by the threat of his weapon. An opponent who attacked regardless (or in ignorance) would find out how quickly the blade could come into play.

Attacks with the longsword, at their most basic, could take the form of powerful two-handed swings that might well crash through a parry or inflict serious injury even through armour. Thrusts driven in by body weight behind the mass of the sword could penetrate even heavy armour, and could be controlled precisely enough to find a weak spot. However, the great strength of the longsword lay in its versatility.

Given the opportunity, the swordsman could make a single all-out swing. Success would be based on good timing and the opponent being either distracted or unable to respond. Such a movement might be made against an opponent who was caught off guard or reeling from an impact, or one heavily engaged with someone else. Against a ready opponent who could defend himself, the swordsman had the option to mix heavy cuts, thrusts and lighter opportunistic slashes.

The 'long edge' of the blade was normally used to cut with, but the 'short edge' (often called the false edge in later systems), which faced the user when the sword was held straight up in front of him, could cut just as well. The body mechanics for a short-edge cut tended to be more awkward and thus not so powerful, but a longswordsman had the option to make a powerful long-edge cut, turn it into a thrust to get past the opponent's defence, and then lay the short edge of his weapon on a weak area and draw the blade towards him for a slicing cut while recovering to a defensive posture.

This ability to attack in so many different ways made the longsword-armed swordsman a dangerous opponent. Against someone armed with a one-handed sword (and no shield), the longswordsman held a clear advantage at both longer measure and also close quarters, where his ability to apply leverage enabled him to overpower the single-handed swordsman or subtly slip past his defence. At middle ranges, both had good options if they could exploit them, but overall the longswordsman had a clear advantage in such a fight.

The longsword was a battlefield weapon, primarily intended for use when in harness. However, it could be used effectively when out of armour. The risks of battling with two-handed weapons while unarmoured were considerable, but the experience was entirely survivable for the skilled or perhaps lucky swordsman. This required a fighting style whereby the sword fully protected the user, and not coincidentally several distinct but equally sophisticated fighting systems emerged.

The earliest known manual on European sword combat is today known rather prosaically as *Manuscript I.33*. Dating from around 1300, it describes a system of defensive postures (or wards) and the various strokes that can be accomplished from them. Studied by historians and historical fencers, this manuscript has been shown by experimentation to contain an effective fighting system of significant sophistication, in contrast to the mindless hacking with gigantic pieces of blunt iron that many still consider medieval combat to have been.

The Great Sword

The great sword was significantly larger than a longsword, sufficiently so that it could not be used in one hand. 'Lesser' weapons such as longswords and bastard swords could deliver an effective one-handed stroke; the great sword was too heavy for this. However, this did not mean that it was clumsy. On the contrary, the great sword was a highly versatile weapon that could adapt to many different circumstances.

The great sword, or zweihänder, grew out of the longsword and initially had a similar form. However, over time it gained additional features, including very long quillions and rings or bars to provide additional hand protection. A section of the blade in front of the main hilt was blunt, and often leather-wrapped, allowing the user to move a hand down the blade when desired. Protection was added in the form of lugs (or flukes) on the blade in front of the secondary grip, preventing an opponent's blade from sliding up into the user's advanced hand.

The great sword could be used conventionally with both hands on the hilt, allowing an immensely powerful swing. Moving the secondary hand down the blade changed the axis of rotation of the weapon and allowed blows to be delivered without much movement. The sword could also be used much in the manner of a staff or a spear, depending on how it was gripped.

This versatility made the great sword a potent weapon in personal combat or on the battlefield. One of its primary uses was against the pike formations that began to dominate European warfare as the late Middle Ages passed into the Renaissance. The pike had fallen out of favour many years previously, but was brought back to the forefront of military strategy by the citizen-soldiers of Switzerland. These often un-armoured men fought on foot in an age of heavily armoured cavalry, and inflicted harsh defeats upon them on several occasions.

The efficiency of the Swiss pikemen was such that they became sought after as mercenaries, and other nations began to copy them. Notable among the rivals of the Swiss were the landsknechts, originally raised by the Holy Roman Empire in 1487 and trained by Swiss instructors. Dense bodies of pike-armed infantry, formed into hedgehogs for defence or charging as a solid mass, quickly came to dominate European warfare. The main problem they presented to their opponents was how to survive the initial contact, to get past the wall of pike points and begin striking at the men holding them.

One answer to this problem, practised by the mercenaries themselves, was to have some men armed with two-handed swords within a pike formation. Just before contact these men would rush out and use their heavy blades to cut a path through the pikes. The great sword was ideal for this purpose; indeed, it might be the only weapon that was really suitable.

The great sword was generally wielded by a big, strong man, who would receive extra pay to reflect his importance and the risks he took. It had enough mass to chop through a pike haft or at least knock it aside; lesser swords might not have possessed the cutting power, or may have simply bounced off a pike haft without moving it aside. An axe or similar weapon might have sufficed, but the great sword's long blade made contact with a pike haft – possibly several – likely, whereas an axe might have contacted with the haft rather than the blade.

Of course, all this was being done in close proximity to the enemy, so the swordsman could expect to be engaged in combat. Here, too, the great sword was ideal for its purpose. With a hand in front of the hilt, the swordsman could deliver killing blows in a very small space – and space was at a premium in the close confines of a 'push of pike'. A swordsman could cut his way into the enemy formation and begin to disrupt it. His versatile weapon had enormous advantages over the pikes held by his enemies, and if they dropped their primary weapons to use daggers or short swords, the great sword was still far superior at close quarters. The best counter was, of course, another great sword.

This combination of pike and great sword proved extremely effective on the battlefields of the sixteenth century. Its downfall came with the prevalence of firearms, which proved, even in their primitive form, lethal against the dense masses of pikemen. In the meantime, the great sword contributed enormously to the effectiveness of the pike-armed formations, and was an enabling factor in their rise to dominance on the battlefield.

Various designs of great sword appeared until, by the mid- to late sixteenth century, it had fallen out of favour in most regions as a battlefield weapon. It survived in ceremonial form long afterwards, and some of these 'parade swords' were extremely fanciful or oversized. This may in part have contributed to the myth that medieval swords were enormously large and heavy. In truth, fighting great swords did not exceed a maximum weight of around 2 kg. This is still quite a lot of metal to be moving around, but a well-constructed great sword was finely balanced so that the 'felt weight', if such a concept exists, would not be very large.

The great sword generally fell out of favour in the later sixteenth century and did not reappear, though its use continued into the seventeenth century in some areas. This notably included Scotland. The Scottish claymore was very much a great sword, though its design fell some way between the longsword and the larger great swords in use on the Continent. It is known to have been used in battle in the last years of the seventeenth century, and probably remained in service for some time after that.

The word claymore is an anglicisation of the Gaelic *claidhaemh-mor*, which is usually translated as 'great sword'. The term has been incorrectly applied to various Scottish swords, notably the basket-hilted broadsword. The claymore proper was of very clean design, with a long (typically 100–120-cm) blade, forward-swept quillions and a long grip.

The great claymore was eventually replaced by another quintessentially Scottish weapon, the basket-hilted broadsword, and the small-sword was also enthusiastically adopted by gentlemen influenced by French fashions. However, this did not occur until the 1700s. In the meantime, a revolution had occurred in sword design and thus swordsmanship.

One-handed swords evolved enormously at the end of the Middle Ages and during the early years of the Renaissance, creating the earliest of what can be considered the 'fencing' swords. These were carried as sidearms and status symbols, and were more for personal defence than battlefield use. However, they did see combat on the battlefield; the Spanish equivalent to the Swiss or German great swordsman was often armed with what was essentially an early rapier and a buckler, and was at times successful in penetrating and disrupting the pike formations of northern European mercenaries.

1 Michael (in white) and Steve (in black) square off with medieval bastard (hand-and-a-half) swords. Both are using high ready positions that give them a range of options. The threat of a strike from a ready sword can be a highly effective defence.

2 With a heavy cutting sword, many defensive actions take the form of a cut into the attack. If Steve begins a downward stroke, Michael's blade is well positioned to cut upward to meet it, deflecting the strike and creating an opening for his own attack.

3 The neutral guard of Terza gives both Michael and myself a wide range of options. It is easy to maintain, as the weight of the weapon rests low and well to the rear. More advanced (extended) guard positions are tiring with a heavy sword such as the rapier.

4 The salute before a bout or duel is a matter of courtesy and respect, a tradition maintained from ancient times to modern sporting competition. Michael and I are using small-swords; our weapons have blunts on the end for safety, but a mask, fencing jacket and gloves would be necessary before any freeplay (essentially sparring with swords) could begin.

5 Not all swords are created equal. My small-sword has a deadly point and can move quickly; Michael's sabre is primarily a cutting weapon that can also thrust. He will probably want to knock my point aside and cut at me, whereas I need to evade his blade and keep my point threatening him. This is not so much a question of which design is 'better' but of which of us can use the features of his weapon to the best advantage.

6 My lunge in the line of Tierce controls Michael's blade by opposing his foible with the forte of my weapon, enabling me to push his blade aside. My hand is high, giving some protection to my face and head if something goes awry.

7 Rather than parrying, I have met Michael's thrust with a counter-attack in opposition. My sword pushes his aside, protecting me and opening the line for my thrust. My rapier hilt protects my head, and my off hand is positioned to provide additional protection if necessary.

8 A thrust with a weapon like the small-sword can be set aside using the unarmed, or 'off', hand. This is possible even with an edged weapon, although the risks are somewhat greater. It is not wise to defend against cuts in this manner.

9 Using a dagger in the off hand to defend gives me additional options. I have carried Michael's thrust far out to the side and counter-attacked at the same time, increasing my chances of landing a thrust while he is committed to his own attack.

10 My rather ill-advised attempt at a cut is easily outreached by Michael's thrust into my lung. Even if I manage to reach him with my strike, he is likely to survive any injury inflicted … whereas a penetrating wound to the chest will probably be fatal.

11 Michael has taken an offensive stance, with his sword side forward. I have responded with a defensive stance, with my left hand forward. Both of us are keeping our daggers well advanced to meet any attack.

12 The essence of using any thrusting weapon, such as the small-sword, is to keep the point aimed at the opponent. Here, I am using the point in line position as a defensive option. Michael needs to clear my weapon before he can move in to attack, or else he will impale himself without any effort on my part.

13 Michael is cutting to my 'inside' line, i.e. the side opposite my sword hand. I have defended with a simple lateral movement of the blade into the line of Quarte. From here I can push my point forward and down to thrust, or make a cut of my own as Michael retracts his spent attack.

14 The 'principle of defence' is to oppose the weak part (foible) of the opponent's blade with the strong part (forte) of your own. I have good control over Michael's blade at this point, as this position gives me the leverage to push it aside when I begin my riposte.

15 Different fighting systems use various terms for it, but the principle is the same; here Michael has 'won the place'. His sword is threatening Steve, whose own weapon is blocked by Michael's blade. Michael can now attack 'safely', i.e. without danger of being struck in return.

16 One of the basic attacks of small-sword fencing (and other styles) is the thrust in Quarte. A high hand position angles the blade to penetrate the chest effectively, and places the sword's handguard to protect my head. This thrust has been made 'in time', i.e. at a moment when my opponent is not attacking me.

17 The moulinet is a rolling action of the blade, which generates force as well as taking the weapon into an open line of attack. Here I begin a moulinet...

18 ...cutting around Michael's blade to deliver a Cut One (diagonally forehand, downwards) to his head and shoulder. This movement is a staple of sabre fencing, and is used with other cutting weapons such as the backsword.

19 Having dummied Michael into defending his head with the Parry of St George, I deliver a Cut Six (horizontal, backhand) to his flank. This movement is one of the most instinctive in all sword systems. My cut is made near the tip of the blade and will be drawn across Michael's abdomen to deliver a slashing injury, rather than trying to shear him in half.

20 Although it is more customary to strike with the sharp part of a sword, the pommel can deliver a powerful blow. It can be jabbed at the opponent without changing grip, or, as here, the weapon can be gripped by the blade and used as a mace. The quillions of the crosspiece may deliver a puncturing wound if they contact the target instead of the pommel.

21 My parry in High Prime is just about to contact Michael's cut. Note the use of the true edge (the main cutting edge) to parry. This is common in most, but not all, European fencing systems. The shell guard (hand guard) of my sabre is well aligned to protect my hand if I have misjudged the parry.

22 Having rather foolishly cut down at the leg – something most sabre systems discourage – I am about to receive a cut to the head. Michael does not need to parry; he has used the simplest of all voids (a leg slip, i.e. moving the leg back out of reach) to make my attack fall short while he remains within striking range.

23 The parry of High Octave is used with heavy-bladed swords such as the backsword or sabre. The blade is allowed to drop under its own weight as the hand is rolled over to point thumb downwards. Retracting the arm creates a defensive barrier that protects the head, flank and sword arm.

24 Michael launches a powerful horizontal cut at my left flank, which I defend by stepping to my right and pivoting to remain facing my opponent. This gets my body weight behind my parry, which catches Michael's cut on the forte of my sabre.

25 As Michael's sabre bounces from my parry, I begin a powerful backhand cut of my own. Michael is already countering with the only defence that will get his blade in the way in time.

26 My cut strikes Michael's parry of High Octave and is stopped. Michael has an obvious riposte from this position, using a backhand cut at my head.

27 I gain time to defend by stepping through with my left foot, moving around the path of the cut, and make a parry in Tierce. From here, the action may continue or we might move apart, ending what is often termed a 'phrase' of the fight.

28 A horizontal overhead parry is called the Parry of St George in many historical fencing systems, presumably because St George is often depicted with his sword in this position. The majority of fencing systems emphasise a solid base and a straight back for most actions; leaning and twisting are used, but care must be taken not to lose balance and become vulnerable.

29 The only way to find out how a rapier and dagger combination would fare against a two-handed sword is to try it. The same goes for any other match-up. Protective equipment includes heavy gloves, Kevlar fencing jacket, body armour or a padded gambeson, fencing mask and an elbow protector. Live blades should not be permitted in the training area, just in case someone makes a tragic mistake.

30 Michael has adopted a resting posture, sometimes called sabre-at-knee; I am using a resting guard commonly associated with the backsword or highland broadsword. Although both of us look quite vulnerable, our weapons can come back into play very quickly.

31 Steve has used the leverage given by his two-handed grip on the sword to lever his weapon around Michael's with enough force to deliver a debilitating cut to the head. Michael's blade is resting on the quillons of Steve's crossguard and thus is under Steve's control for long enough for him to make his strike.

32 In many, but by no means all, sword systems, the various guard positions are used to close off some of the opponent's lines of attack, limiting his options. My weapon is not very well positioned here. It is angled inwards and is not really covering any of the possible lines of attack.

33 This enables Michael to simply thrust straight through my guard. If I thought I was covered in that line, I would likely be caught by surprise by an attack there. With a weapon that moves as fast as the small-sword, there is no time to recover from being caught off guard in this manner.

34 Body movement is highly important when fighting with heavy swords such as the rapier. Here I have gained time to defend by transferring my weight backwards on to the rear leg, moving 'vita' and everything above it away from the attack.

35 Having deflected Michael's thrust and gained control of his blade, I transfer my weight forward again without moving my feet, gaining reach without changing the distance between us. I do not need to – Michael closed in to attack and has not yet retreated, so I am well within reach to strike him.

36 Michael and Steve are half-swording. As the name suggests, the left hand is about halfway down the blade, turning the sword into a short staff-like weapon. Half-sword can be used to increase the strength of a defence or to knock a blade aside…

37 ...or it can be used to guide and increase the power of a thrust. Here Michael has gone 'off the line' to find an opening, and driven in a thrust that would be sufficiently powerful to defeat many forms of armour.

38 Steve could have countered Michael's half-sword attack by positioning the tip of his own blade to deflect the thrust and leaving it there to protect him while he struck a deadly close-quarters blow with the heavy pommel.

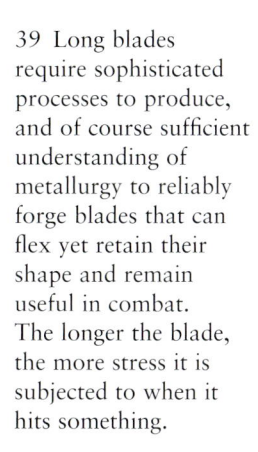

39 Long blades require sophisticated processes to produce, and of course sufficient understanding of metallurgy to reliably forge blades that can flex yet retain their shape and remain useful in combat. The longer the blade, the more stress it is subjected to when it hits something.

40 The Under Stop Lunge is a void executed by extending the back leg rearwards and dropping low, much like a lunge in reverse. Michael's attack goes over my head as he steps on to my outstretched point.

41 Steve parries Michael's cut, taking his left hand off the hilt of his sword as soon as he feels the contact of blades.

42 Keeping his sword as a barrier to prevent Michael's weapon from cutting him, Steve wraps his arm around the blade. He must prevent Michael from wrenching the blade backwards by getting a good grip on it as quickly as possible.

43 Michael's blade must slide in order to cut Steve. He does not give it the chance to do so, taking it out of Michael's hands by rotating the left side of his torso backwards.

44 The same movement also facilitates a one-handed cut, which will probably end the fight. If not, Michael has no weapon and would be well advised to surrender.

45 Michael has caught me off guard, thinking I am out of measure and thus safe, when in fact I am within range of a lunge. The lunge is used in many fencing systems, although there are significant variations in some. Michael's back foot remains in place, his extending left leg driving him forward to increase his reach. Michael will recover backwards out of his lunge, returning to his original position.

46 Facing a two-handed sword is sufficiently intimidating that I felt the need to support my rapier parry with my dagger at this juncture. The psychological factors make armed combat much more than a chess game with swords, but without hands-on experience it is not really possible to understand how important they are.

47 'Dual Wielding' is depicted in many games and movies as being an extremely potent form of combat. In reality, silly tricks like double inward swiping attacks are little more than assisted suicide. Had I kept one weapon back to defend and used the other to strike, I would have had an advantage. Instead I am about to receive a well-deserved sword to the head.

48 Although the length of the sword permits fighting at quite long measure, it is sometimes advantageous to close in. Steve has stepped right in and jammed Michael's sword where it cannot harm him, leaving his own in a rather more threatening position.

49 Double cuts from the same side are another 'dual wielding' trick portrayed as somehow more effective than the swordplay that was actually used in combat. My double cut has been parried by a single blade; my best option now is to use one weapon to defend against Michael's riposte and the other to make a new attack. A double-sword parry at this point would be simply ridiculous.

50 After their blades meet, Michael takes one hand off the hilt and uses the pommel of his weapon as a hook, trying to catch Steve's wrists. This will enable him to drag Steve forward and off balance.

51 Michael's free hand pushes Steve's arm to prevent him turning to defend himself. Michael can now push his weapon forward into Steve's face and neck, and draw or push a cut. He also has the option to use a throw from this position; many medieval fighting systems included significant amounts of wrestling to back up the sword techniques.

CHAPTER 5

The Art of Defence: Swords of the Renaissance

There are rarely any hard and fast boundaries in history. There have been few events, if any, that were so pivotal that a new era began instantly afterward. Instead, history is a shifting pattern of advance, stagnation and occasional collapse, and of course conditions vary from one place to another. By way of example, the 'Viking Era' is considered to have ended at Hastings in 1066, but the people of Iceland, or those that were at the time establishing a colony in Greenland, probably did not notice.

So it was with the Renaissance. Defined by a cultural change, it is harder than usual to find start and end points for the Renaissance as a period in history as opposed to a snapshot of the culture of the time. That said, the Renaissance is usually considered to have begun in Florence in the fourteenth century and gradually spread out from there. Exactly who had embraced the Renaissance and who was still living in the Middle Ages in any given year is a difficult question to answer. What is clear is that society gradually changed across Europe, and in very significant ways.

The Renaissance was characterised by new directions in art (such as the use of perspective) and a resurgence of scholarship. Geniuses such as Leonardo da Vinci produced great works at an alarming rate, and the very values by which people judged themselves began to change. This may have in part arisen out of the enormous death toll caused by bubonic plague, also known as the Black Death.

The plague reached Europe in 1347, carried by fleas feeding on rats aboard ships. It entered Europe by way of Messina in Sicily, and soon broke out in other ports. From there it spread rapidly, killing rich and poor indiscriminately. The effects were worse in crowded and unsanitary cities, but no area was safe. So many died that there were not enough priests to give the last rites – the Pope decreed that anyone who died of the plague would be considered to have received the appropriate rites.

The social and economic devastation arising out of the Black Death facilitated great changes in Europe. So many workers had died that labour was for once a commodity in great demand. Common farmworkers could move from one employer to another seeking better wages and conditions, giving them a freedom previously unheard of. Similarly, the social order was disrupted to the point where ambitious people could rise to power or greatness in fields as diverse as art, science and politics.

The Renaissance is usually considered to have reached France around 1494, though many of the cultural ideas that underpinned it were already known there. War with England (the Hundred Years War, actually running from 1337 to 1453) and the ravages of the plague put France in a poor economic position, so that the Renaissance only reached its height in France after 1515 or so.

A similar situation existed in England. The commonly accepted start date for England is 1485, i.e. the return of stability following the end of the Wars of the Roses. However, although Henry VIII of England was something of a Renaissance man, Renaissance ideas were in general relatively slow to take hold in England. It was not really until the reign of Queen Elizabeth I, beginning in 1558, that England really entered the new age. Thus many Renaissance concepts tend to be referred to as 'Elizabethan' in Britain.

The Renaissance, then, was not an abrupt social change or a sharply defined period in history. By the mid- to late 1500s, most people in Europe could be considered to be living in Renaissance society, and Renaissance values were well established. One reason for this was the written – or, more importantly, printed – word.

The introduction of relatively fast and reliable printing allowed scholarship to become far more widespread than previously, and also permitted those with strong ideas (be they right, wrong or very strange indeed) to make them available to the masses. The most famous of these early printed books was the Gutenberg Bible, which went into production around 1450, but as time went on more and more books began to be printed. Some were on science and philosophy, some on more obscure topics, and some were on the subject of swordsmanship.

Often known as treatises or *Fechtbücher* (fighting books), these manuals had existed before the introduction of movable type printing, but the expense involved in creating and disseminating a *Fechtbuch* was enormously reduced. Many fencing masters laid down their thoughts in manuals, which vary greatly in quality.

Some, such as Capoferro's 1610 work on rapier fencing, feature useful illustrations that are artworks in their own right, along with a logical approach to armed combat. Others are cheaply produced and far less well presented, with badly drawn illustrations that do not always match the text and/or impenetrable verbiage that obfuscates what might otherwise be a quite simple concept. The mere fact that a treatise has survived to this day does not mean it contains good information, nor that it is likely to be useful to the student of fencing.

One recurring theme in the fencing manual is that while they usually explain what is to be done in order to achieve a given result, details on how this is accomplished are often sketchy. This is largely because a treatise was not a 'how-to' manual for beginners. It was in part a statement of the master's opinions on how to fence and in part a sort of advertisement for his services. Essentially, the reader was being told, 'I can teach you how to do all of these amazing things, if you are willing to give me a suitable sum of money.'

The typical treatise, no matter how badly written or confusing, explains at great length why the master writing it is the very best in the business, and how his system is superior to all others. Often a simple concept, such as how to parry a thrust, will be buried in a great diatribe on why certain foreign systems are inferior, or a lengthy discourse on why this master knows better than anyone else how to defeat those poor benighted fools who follow other systems.

Rampant egomania and xenophobia often leap from the pages, at times confusing the poor reader to the point where the mechanics of a stroke cannot be fathomed. One is moved to wonder if this was the point in some cases – the aim being to present a tantalising glimpse of something that appears to be very good but remains beyond the ken of the reader. The only answer, of course, was to ask the master to show how it was done.

Today, we do not have the luxury of doing so. Fencing systems must be painstakingly reconstructed by experimentation using manuals, translated from an archaic form of a foreign language, which were not all that clear in the first place. This leads to a certain amount of disagreement among scholars and historical fencers about exactly how a given master executed a particular technique.

These masters were not short of opinions to push on the reader, nor of ink with which to write them. Some manuals are interesting as examples of the thinking of the time, whether or not they were any use as a *Fechtbuch*. Quirky styles include the practice of writing the entire manual like a play, with master and pupil having a conversation in which the student, who is often stunningly dim-witted, asks a variety of questions to which the master provides long-winded (and only sometimes useful) answers. These are of course liberally studded with contempt for other systems and a general mistrust of foreigners.

Some of the questions are particularly stupid, and serve mainly to illustrate how clever and learned the master is – at least in comparison to a feeble-minded buffoon. This can make quite entertaining reading, but it provides little assistance to the student seeking to fathom the mysteries of the master's system. It must be remembered that this was likely never the master's intent; his treatise was designed to attract the patronage of rich and powerful men or possibly an attempt to assert his status among the fencing masters of the era. If it allowed students to learn his system without him, it might actually harm his business.

Within the pages of these works, however badly obfuscated by verbiage and xenophobia, are the thoughts of learned and experienced men who – in the fashion of the time – had applied logic and reason to the study of swordsmanship. Science was burgeoning in the era, and was applied to the noble art of fighting with a sword. Thus we see indications of precise angles and measured movements, designed to confound an opponent, which will, we are assured, lead to certain victory if the underlying geometrical principles are applied correctly. Since art was flourishing to an equal degree at the time, we also see backgrounds depicting Bible scenes, cherubs, animals and the occasional burning ship.

The relevance of these embellishments is dubious at best; at times they confuse the eye and make illustrations harder to comprehend than is really necessary. Yet they serve to illustrate the spirit of the times, and thus may be necessary to comprehension of the specifics. In order to understand a fighting system, it is necessary to study its wider context. The clothing of the era, the social conditions and the sort of tasks familiar to students of the system all influence it, as does the general ethos of the age. Although Renaissance fencing manuals can make it hard to figure out the details, the big picture is right there on the page. Without that big picture, many of the specifics would make no sense at all.

The Art of Defence

A certain fencing instructor is fond of remarking that the first rule of sword fighting is 'stay alive long enough to win'. The second rule is that 'at some point you will have to do something bad to the opponent'. However, the urgency of fulfilling rule two and thus winning the fight must never overwhelm the necessity of obeying rule one.

Outside of movies and television, where wounds have the effects that the director wants them to have, it is very rare that any sword thrust or stroke will instantly disable an opponent. Shearing off or crippling an arm beyond use, or decapitating the opponent, will prevent him from returning the blow, but even a lethal cut or thrust may well leave the victim with a few seconds of life in which to avenge himself. He may fold up around the wound, but in the adrenalised state of a fight he may not be fully aware of what has just happened to him. Worse, he may know and be enraged. His last moments could be spent in a berserk rage, piling into his slayer with no regard for his personal safety, as that has just become meaningless.

There is also the prospect that the swordsman might misjudge his attack and receive a blow while launching one of his own, or run on to a stop cut or the point of a weapon held 'point in line', i.e. aimed right at him. After a successful defence, he might fall foul of an incompetent or reckless opponent who immediately tries to jab or cut again – the term for this is a remise – rather than defending himself against the inevitable counter. In the fencing world, there is a well-known adage: 'If you are hit because of the opponent's good fencing, congratulate him. If you are hit because of his bad fencing, berate yourself.'

In a fight with live weapons, it does not matter whether the swordsman is hit due to good or bad fencing; hit is hit and injured is injured. Thus the fencing systems of the Renaissance (and in truth, all good fighting systems) emphasised defence first and foremost. This is the origin of the term 'fencing'. It comes from 'art of defence', which refers to the paramount function of skill at arms: survival.

In practical terms, the Renaissance fencing masters set out systems whereby the opponent was denied an opportunity for an attack so far as was possible. The swordsman could then manoeuvre for an advantage that would allow him to attack 'safely'. This apparently strange term simply means that the swordsman can attack without exposing himself to the risk of being hit in return. Preparations for doing so are variously referred to as 'winning the line' or 'winning the place', which essentially means getting control of the opponent's blade or limiting his options to prevent any counter.

Various methods of doing so were put forward by different masters. Movement, either in the form of altering the distance between the combatants or circling to move off the line of attack, was one option. Another was voiding the attack by dodging just enough to make it miss while launching a counterstroke. A parry followed by a riposte was another option, or counter-attacking in such a way that the action closed the opponent's line of attack and acted as defence as well as wounding him.

A parry and riposte is referred to as a two-tempi action, i.e. it takes two 'periods of fencing time': one to deflect or block the attack and another to launch a counterstroke. A counterstroke that is also a defensive action is a single-tempo action, in that it takes one period of fencing time to execute a single movement. In both cases the swordsman had to ensure not only that he stopped the opponent's attack but also that he prevented the opponent from succeeding, with an immediate follow-up that might result in both combatants being struck.

The line, or place, could also be won by preparatory movements. These included attacks on the blade, such as beating it aside with a sharp rap of the swordsman's weapon, and takings of the blade such as the bind, whereby the opponent's blade was moved and held where the swordsman wanted it using his own weapon.

These various movements – attacks, parries, voids, takings of the blade and attacks on the blade – are generally considered to constitute fencing, but in truth they are merely the means by which the art of defence is made to work. Fencing itself is simply the art of hitting without being hit; all else is detail. With this in mind, it is hardly surprising that a wide range of fencing styles emerged in the Renaissance, all geared towards the same end result but often using rather different methods to achieve it.

The Estoc and the Tuck Sword

The estoc emerged in the fourteenth century, a product of the need to penetrate heavy armour. It was a long-bladed sword of simple design, with no cutting edge. This was largely due to the blade cross section, which was typically triangular, square or rhomboid to create a stiff blade capable of punching through armour. Most estocs had a longsword-like hilt, i.e. they could be used in both hands, but were employed in a very versatile manner. An estoc could be used as a short lance from horseback, driven home by the mass of a moving horse.

A swordsman on foot and armed with an estoc might use it with one or both hands on the hilt, thrusting in the manner of a longsword. Indeed, the word estoc derives from the French for thrust. However, the weapon could be held half-sword (i.e. with one hand on the blade) and used much like a staff. The pommel and crosspiece made an effective bludgeoning instrument, while the quillions could be used to hook, pull or trip an opponent. Thus estoc fighting at times resembled armoured wrestling with sharp-ended staves. One sure method of obtaining a killing blow was to cause the opponent to fall and then plunge the estoc into him, with one hand on the hilt and one on the blade, or both on the blade.

The estoc was known by other names elsewhere in Europe. In England it was known as a tuck, which is apparently a corruption of estoc. The Italian version was known as the stocco. These weapons remained in service until the seventeenth century, but became less prevalent as the need to penetrate heavy armour was reduced by its absence from the battlefield.

The estoc, or tuck, was very much a battle sword rather than a 'fencing' weapon in the usual sense of that word. However, estoc fighting systems followed the principles of the art of defence; there is no difference in concept between an armoured man throwing his opponent to the ground and then finishing him when he cannot reply and a rapier fencer's rather more elegant winning of the place by taking and carrying the opponent's blade off line and then delivering a fatal thrust.

The estoc did not evolve into later 'fencing'-type swords as such, but neither did it simply fade away. Instead, many of the principles of using the estoc found their way into the emerging disciplines of what today would be recognised as rapier fencing. The estoc was the first primarily (or exclusively, if you ignore the wrestling and use as a hammer or staff) thrusting sword to see widespread use for almost a thousand years. However, it emerged to deal with heavy armour, which was in decline, and so gradually was replaced with weapons more suitable to the needs of the day.

The Espada Ropera and the Spada da Lato

The espada ropera and spada da lato can be considered forerunners of the rapier, though both remained in use at the same time as true rapiers were in service. Their evolution was by way of the medieval arming sword, which was given additional hand protection in the form of rings to prevent the opponent's blade from sliding up and injuring the wielder's hand.

Notably, this additional protection included a section in front of the crosspiece, creating an enclosed and protected ricasso. This in turn allowed the user to place one or sometimes two fingers over the crosspiece, altering the balance of the weapon and facilitating certain movements without exposing the finger to the risk of being severed.

The spada da lato is more commonly known as the sidesword in modern parlance, probably in the context of it being a sidearm. It was a primarily civilian weapon, carried for personal defence, rather than a battlefield tool. At the time it was in use, a variety of great swords, pikes and pole arms of many sorts were available for large-scale combat, along with matchlock and, later, wheel-lock firearms. An officer might carry his sidesword to a battle, but his weapon of choice was a regiment of pikemen or a force of musketeers; he would not expect or intend to fight it out with the enemy using his sword.

The sidesword became prevalent in Italy, notably among the fencing masters of Bologna. These apparently taught a very similar system to one another, and it has become known as the Dardi school after Lippo Bartolomeo Dardi. Dardi founded his fencing school in 1415, and in many ways incorporated both the late medieval concepts of swordsmanship and the emerging ideas of the Renaissance. Some modern scholars tend to include heavy military rapiers in with sideswords, and often refer to them as such, though arguably the whole group of rapier-like weapons can be subdivided in a variety of other ways, and forms a distinct (but very broad) general type that evolved over time and according to local influences.

The espada ropera, or 'dress sword', originated in Spain at around the same time as the Italian sidesword was appearing, and was broadly similar in terms of form and function. Like the sidesword, the espada ropera was primarily intended for use when in civilian dress, i.e. out of armour and thus not on a battlefield. Both weapons gained an increasing amount of hand protection over time, until the few rings of the early sidesword had become the complex swept hilt of the rapier.

The environment in which these weapons were used was typically urban, crowded, and cramped. Swords might be drawn over all manner of petty disputes, and fights would take place on uncertain footing, such as cobbles made slippery by filth from chamber pots or passing horses. The streets of the times were ill-lit at night. All this meant that mobility was a questionable asset; a long lunge could result in lost footing, or a rapid retirement in the face of an attack could lead to the swordsman tripping over something or crashing into a wall.

Thus, linear movement was not necessarily desirable. The fighting systems of the early Renaissance emphasised circling movements instead, enabling the fencer to see where he was putting his feet while moving himself out of the way of an attack. The heavy-bladed sidesword or espada ropera could deliver a powerful cut or a deadly thrust, but it was somewhat slow on the defence. Trying to parry in the manner of a lighter sword was not a good option, so to a great extent sidesword technique utilised a system whereby the swordsman moved around his weapon.

Rather than taking the sword to where it needed to be in order to parry an attack, the swordsman would move himself away from the attack, leaving the sword as a barrier. This seems counter-intuitive to those who have studied later fencing systems, but in the context of a sidesword fight in a dark, cobbled alley outside a Shakespearean theatre it was highly effective.

Sidesword fencing was greatly concerned with winning the line, or place, and not committing to any action unless it was highly likely to succeed. Hot-headed opponents could easily be despatched with a fairly minimal movement, but one who kept his cool and ensured his sword was always a threat was much harder to deal with. For this reason, sophisticated combination techniques were taught by the fencing masters, enabling the well-trained swordsman to force a lesser opponent into making a mistake that would leave him open.

Many of the sidesword masters also taught dancing; many dances of the era used the same footwork as swordsmanship. Indeed, it was said that you should not give a sword to a man who could not dance. Some of the footwork associated with the sidesword has survived into the modern era, concealed within the (usually) rather less violent world of ballet.

The sidesword could be employed in conjunction with defensive weapons such as a dagger or a cloak wrapped around the unarmed arm, with enough left dangling to entangle the opponent's weapon. A buckler or small shield could also be used. Men armed in this manner were fielded by the Spanish as a counter to the pike- and great-sword-armed forces that at the time dominated European warfare, and later, as the pike and musket came to be the primary battlefield combination, these sword-and-bucklermen were used as flank guards and skirmishers to protect the potent but unwieldy pike and musket formations.

Among the key techniques of the sidesword was the use of body weight to drive a thrust and to push aside an opponent's blade. Rather than extending the sword arm straight forward, many sidesword techniques held it out to the side, creating a triangle with the point angled inward. Performed in opposition, i.e. in contact with the opponent's blade, this movement pushed his weapon away from the swordsman, making the attack safer. Forward motion of the body delivered force into the opponent by way of the triangle formed by arm and sword, the axis of the attack being the third side of the triangle.

Although the sidesword had the mass to deliver a powerful shearing cut, it did not rely on purely percussive blows. Instead, a cut was delivered percussively, focusing the impact of the weapon behind a sharp edge, and was then drawn to pull as much blade as possible through the wound thus caused. As the blade cleared the target, it could be driven forward again, following the cut with a thrust. This would push the victim away from the swordsman, reducing the chances of a return blow made before the shock of injury registered.

The sidesword's weight meant that it punished mistakes; a swordsman who allowed his weapon to wander off line or who lost control of it would be quickly killed or disabled by a more disciplined opponent. Caution was extremely important in a fight if the swordsman did not wish to compromise himself. There was another dimension to this; a lot of 'sword fights' were actually stand-offs in which no serious blows were struck.

As a dispute became heated and weapons were drawn, the opponents would circle one another, seeking an opening and trying to deny the opponent one. It was entirely possible that neither actually wanted to kill the other, whether for moral reasons, because it might lead to a feud with their family, or to avoid legal issues arising from having killed a man over a trivial matter.

The problem at this point was that it might be socially unacceptable to back down, losing face before the onlookers, once swords were drawn, and in any case the swordsman could not be sure that his opponent was not intent upon murder. Attempting to temporise in the middle of a sword fight could be fatal. The only answer was to fight and not lose. Winning, in the sense of harming or killing the opponent, might not be the goal at all, but could turn out to be necessary.

In a stand-off of this sort, if one fencer left an opening then the other really had to make an attempt to strike him. To do otherwise might seem cowardly and damage the fencer's reputation. However, in many cases a well-trained fencer could contrive to look threatening and dangerous for long enough that his friends might 'persuade' him not to kill his adversary, or someone might shout that the watch was coming and cause everyone to scatter or pretend that nothing was happening. Onlookers would remember a nasty sword fight, with blades moving around one another with deadly intent as two fencers tried to win the place and deliver a killing thrust. Fortunately the fight was broken up before anybody got killed!

Some fights would end in death or severe injury of course, but greater skill on either or both sides made it more likely that someone who did not really wish to kill would not have to. A desperate man would have to take any opportunity to strike his opponent and end the matter, while one who was well in control of the situation had more options. This satisfied rule one – stay alive long enough to win – since winning is defined as surviving the encounter. What happens to the opponent is always secondary to emerging alive from the fight.

The Rapier

The term 'rapier' can refer to a great variety of weapons, and in some cases includes sideswords. Numerous designs emerged throughout the weapon's career, with blade lengths typically in the 90- to 120-cm range. Longer weapons were at times used, either as duelling weapons or status symbols. A very long blade would make the weapon impossible to draw quickly, which was not a problem in a prearranged duel but could be fatal in a sudden street assault.

Very long blades were at times associated with braggarts and troublemakers. In Elizabethan England, a certain kind of young man would carry a rapier whose blade was 'longer than a yard' and would wear a ruff that was also excessively large. Orders were given that these troublemakers were to be arrested and their ruff or blade cut down to a more acceptable length. The financial impact of this must have been enormous – longer blades required the highest quality of sword-making, which did not come cheap.

The main differences between a rapier and a sidesword were the lighter, thinner blade of the rapier and the more complex hilt. The thinner blade arose out of a move from cut-and-thrust fighting to emphasis on the thrust, with the cut as a secondary expedient. Some rapiers were sharpened only from halfway down the blade, some for all of their length, but all were optimised for the thrust. A variant, with a blade more suited to cutting, was sometimes referred to as a 'sword rapier'.

Over time, fashions changed and blades became longer or shorter, wider or narrower. Specialist variants included weapons with a widened blade near the tip, for the purpose of making opportunistic tip cuts more effectively. Although unlikely to disable an opponent, a cut of this sort would bloody him, ending a duel to first blood. It would also weaken the opponent or impede him by causing blood from a cut above the eye to blind him. It might even sever tendons and disable the opponent.

Hilts also continued to evolve. The swept hilt offered good hand protection in the form of a knuckle bow, a system of rings and bars in front of the hand, and quillions to catch a blade. More complex, intricate and/or beautiful versions gradually emerged, usually but not always increasing hand protection. This found its ultimate expression in the cup-hilted rapier, which retained quillions but replaced the elegant web of rings and bars with a rather dowdy – though sometimes beautifully engraved – cup of metal that enclosed the front of the user's hand.

A nice-looking rapier was a status symbol, and was especially important in court circles. The quality of the blade, and its effectiveness in a fight, was not always as important, and many rapiers were bought as dress items rather than weapons. That said, high-quality weaponry was well respected in most areas. Blades from Toledo in Spain were famous for their quality, so much so that they were mentioned in several of Shakespeare's plays.

The main rival for the title of greatest centre of European sword-making was Solingen, in Westphalia. Solingen grew into a fortified city in the fifteenth century, and remained a major centre for high-quality blades thereafter, but during the Renaissance it was a Toledo blade that would attract the most admiration from the owner's peers.

Prowess with the rapier was the hallmark of the gentleman, and an essential skill to be acquired by the socially ambitious. It is likely that possession of the latest fencing treatise, and the ability to discuss or dismiss its contents in an apparently knowledgeable fashion, was also a must-have social accessory. So was being able to claim that the swordsman was the student of a well-respected fencing master.

There was of course enormous rivalry between different schools of fence, not least because the income from teaching well-off gentlemen and members of the nobility was considerable. Masters had to claim to be the best, to know secrets that others did not and so forth, in order to retain their students and attract the right sort of new ones – i.e. rich men.

One curious development arising out of this situation was the different forms of salute used by the various fencing schools. The salute probably had its origins in the knightly habit of raising the sword, blade pointing straight up, and kissing the hilt before engaging in combat or when swearing an oath. Courtesy was extremely important in the Renaissance, even between sworn enemies who hated one another, and so a salute with the sword before combat became a social requirement.

The salute served another purpose; it was a declaration of what the swordsman brought to the fight. If his off hand was empty, this would be demonstrated, whereas if he had brought a dagger, buckler or other off-hand tool he was declaring it openly to ensure a fair fight. The salute began with the arms down and palms towards the opponent, and then proceeded in a manner decreed by the master who taught the swordsman. The salute would incorporate some variant on raising the blade straight up and/or pointing it at the opponent being saluted, and might be quite complex.

The mutual salute served to demonstrate that both combatants were ready to fight, ensuring that there could be no claims of ambush or murder afterward, and declared what weapons each had about his person. It also indicated who taught the swordsman, which could bring matters to a close or escalate them. Some masters had a reputation for producing excellent fencers, which could intimidate someone who had been instructed by a lesser individual or who feared the secret techniques said to be taught behind closed doors.

Of course, encounters between members of rival schools could be more intense because of the reputations involved or previous bloody encounters. At times, the situation might have resembled a 1970s kung fu movie (though probably with less squawking) as the rivals postured and insulted one another's fencing style, their master, their sword, their relatives and probably their dress sense too. Brawls between members of rival fencing schools were as much a problem as any other sort of feud, and just as bloody.

In addition to differences in the system put forward by various individual fencing masters, there were very distinct regional styles. The most notable of these were the Italian and Spanish styles, which emerged gradually over time. The Italian school, as it is known, included a number of highly influential masters, such as Dardi, Agrippa, di Grassi, Saviolo, Fabris and Capoferro.

The Italian school was, to a great extent, the forerunner of modern fencing. It incorporated movements such as the lunge, and emphasised the thrust in a manner that looks and feels familiar to the modern student of Olympic-style fencing. There are significant differences of course, not least because the Renaissance rapier was much longer and heavier than a modern sporting épée or foil. The Italian-school rapier fencer also had to consider that his opponent could cut as well as thrust, and might not be matched against an identical weapon. However, the lineage of modern fencing can be traced back to the Italian school of rapier fencing.

The Spanish system was rather different. Often referred to as Destreza (literally, 'skill'), the Spanish school was more than a rapier fighting system; indeed it was more than a fighting system of any sort. Spanish fencers were educated in the works of classical scholars and were particularly interested in geometry as well as what today is called biomechanics. Rather than lunging at his opponent, the Spanish rapier fencer manoeuvred on the 'mysterious circle', which was defined by the reach of the combatants and the length of their swords.

By correct use of the angles created by his sword and that of the opponent, a fencer could – in theory – create a winning position by use of geometry. This was in some ways similar to certain aspects of sidesword play, but the Spanish fencer presented his weapon at arm's length, pointed at the opponent to keep him at a respectful distance. This required long practice to develop the strength needed to maintain the position, but once established it denied the opponent much in the way of a target.

The mysterious circle was something of a philosophical concept, and one very much a product of the Renaissance way of thinking. This merging of practical swordsmanship and what amounts to mysticism in some way parallels aspects of some Oriental martial arts, and it is equally hard to see where combat effectiveness ends and abstruse philosophical concepts begin.

The Destreza method was highly effective, and was influential beyond Europe – it was taught wherever Spanish explorers and colonists found themselves. However, over time it was increasingly influenced (some would say corrupted) by more mainstream fencing methods, and gradually faded away. As a result, the Spanish school did not have much influence on later sword-fighting systems, although many later masters included ways of dealing with 'a Spaniard' in their work.

This sort of reference to a scholar of a regional fencing system by a presumed nationality can be confusing to the modern reader. It is essentially shorthand, and does not mean that the master thought that all Spaniards would attack in a certain manner while all Italians were obsessed with a particular, different, set of strokes. Rather, it suggested that a student of that school of fencing (who was quite likely but not certain to be of the mentioned nationality) probably fenced in a certain way.

German and French schools of rapier fencing did exist, but they were of relatively minor importance compared to the Italian style, which heavily influenced or eclipsed them. The English style was also heavily influenced by Italian thinking, but in some cases displayed a different emphasis. The system put forward by Vincentio Saviolo in 1595 is one of the earliest books on fencing written in English (though this does not make it especially easy to comprehend) and was highly influential. An Italian, Saviolo's style was heavily based in Italian thinking of the time, and was challenged by other English masters. George Silver was a particularly savage critic.

Another notable English master was Joseph Swetnam, whose manual included lengthy discourse on social matters in addition to offering advice on fencing with the rapier and other weapons. Swetnam advocated fencing from long measure, using thrusts made on the lunge, in a style influenced by the Italian school but drawing heavily on contemporary English thinking. Swetnam was also noted for publishing poisonous tracts vilifying women in general, and for (probably falsely) claiming that he had been fencing instructor to the deceased Henry, Prince of Wales.

Most famous of the English fencing masters is George Silver, whose 1599 work *Paradoxes of Defence* deals largely with the (real or imagined) evils of rapiers, foreign rapier masters, and foreigners in general. Amid his oft-stated xenophobia, Silver contends that the rapier does not grant the user much protection, and that false foreign systems were far too concerned with offence than with first securing the safety of the swordsman and only then offending against the opponent.

Silver did put forward four key principles of fencing, which are all interrelated. He advocated that the fencer be mindful of measure (i.e. distance between himself and the opponent), which in turn affected the time available to defend against an incoming strike or required for a blow to reach the target. This was modified by consideration of the place, which can be taken to mean the situation at any given moment in a fight.

All of these factors had to be considered with what is probably the most important of Silver's 'four governors': judgement. Foreigners and rapier fencers might charge in regardless of the situation, but according to Silver, an Englishman would be more careful about when and how he exposed himself to harm, using his judgement of the situation to determine when to strike so that he might win without exposing himself to undue risk.

Silver was not alone in espousing these factors as the key to good and 'safe' fencing. Others might phrase them differently, but they remain relevant. Place, in particular, is a key concept. It will take a blade a certain amount of time to cross a certain distance. How long depends on the weapon itself – some move faster than others, and some are too heavy to change direction quickly – and the swordsman holding it. A swordsman whose stance is sloppy will take longer to get moving, and will advertise his movements more than one who is well poised, which in turn affects how long it will take for his blow to arrive. Similarly, the attitude of the blades is a factor. If the opponent's blade must be cleared out of the way, or the attack must go around it, then this will take longer than a direct thrust.

Thus, depending on the situation (or place), it is possible at times to be very close to the opponent and yet in no danger, since he cannot reach you in the time it will take you to defend, and at other times to be positioned to strike an opponent knowing that he cannot react quickly enough to save himself. An appreciation of measure (or distance), time and place allows the fencer to recognise when a movement is a threat and when it is not, which can help protect against falling for feints or being forced to give up an advantageous position due to an imaginary threat. Conversely, it permits the fencer to judge when he could be in real trouble and to take appropriate action.

Fighting with the Rapier Alone

The rapier was long and heavy, and could not change direction as quickly as a lighter sword. On the other hand it possessed the mass to push aside a defensive action and the reach to injure an opponent from a respectable distance. As noted elsewhere, it was optimised for the thrust but could also cut with either of its two long edges. The Italian school strongly emphasised the thrust; the Spanish considered both cut and thrust to be more or less equally important.

Leading with a cut was a risky action with the rapier, since cutting required a closer measure than thrusting. It was likely that the fencer would be run through before his cut could land, unless he preceded it with an action such as a thrust to cover his closing of measure. Cuts could be made as powerful percussive actions; although the rapier did not have the blade mass of heavier weapons such as the sidesword, it did possess enough mass to make the edge bite deep into the target. Drawing the cut then widened and deepened the wound, which might be enough to disable the opponent and would certainly weaken him.

Lighter, some would go so far as to say sneaky, tip cuts could also be used to weaken and wear down an opponent. A tip cut was, as the name suggests, a slicing action made using just the end few centimetres of blade, with a small movement that generated little force. Although a tip cut was unlikely to disable the opponent, nobody likes being slashed about the arm, body or face. The threat might be enough to make the opponent react the way the swordsman wanted, and thus could open him up for a more decisive action.

However, the rapier was primarily designed to thrust into the opponent, and to do so from a considerable distance. Thrusts were usually made in opposition, though some styles varied in their approach. Opposition means that the blades were engaged, pressing against one another, and the thrust held the opponent's weapon away from the swordsman or even pushed it aside. Engagement was almost always with the true edge, i.e. the 'outer' edge of the blade that faces the opponent if the sword is held pointing straight up. Using the true edge kept the hand aligned in its strongest position and applied force more effectively than using the false edge, though this was also possible.

The rapier was best suited to single-tempo actions, in which the opponent's attack was defeated in the same action as the counter was made. Such actions might include a thrust in opposition, made against the opponent's attack to clear it and return the strike in a single movement. Two-tempo actions such as a distinct parry and riposte might be more appropriate against a cut than a thrust. Alternatively the fencer could set aside a thrust (but not a cut) by pushing it away with the empty off hand while making a counter-attack with the rapier.

Some rapier systems made extensive use of the lunge, while others did not. The lunge had the advantage of generating great force, which would drive the rapier point deep into the opponent, but it did leave the fencer vulnerable if his attack failed and he did not recover quickly from his lunge. Performed correctly, the lunge allowed the fencer to gain ground, extending the reach of his thrust, while keeping the back foot firmly planted. Pushing back with the front foot facilitated a quick recovery to the starting position, preserving the original measure. Alternatively, if the opponent retired in the face of attack the fencer could bring his back foot forward to resume a normal stance, effectively advancing by means of the lunge.

A common fault when lunging (in all fencing systems) is to throw the head and the upper body forward, which leads to the fencer landing with too much weight on the front foot and his body structure compromised. This in turn makes it difficult to recover in time to avoid being hit, and not coincidentally makes the fencer's attack less likely to succeed. A good lunge does not throw the upper body forward but instead moves the centre of gravity, referred to as 'vita', closer to the opponent, while retaining good alignment of the upright (or more or less upright) torso.

Historically, attitudes to leaning on the lunge varied. Some systems absolutely forbade any leaning whatsoever, retaining a fully upright position. Others permitted a certain amount of lean to gain some extra reach, and some used a very considerable amount of upper-body movement. However, in all cases this came from the core of the body (i.e. vita) rather than being a flinging forward of the head, and was done in a biomechanically sound manner that preserved good body structure and thus the ability to return to a guard position as needed.

The pass can be used instead of the lunge, and is preferred to it in some systems. In an attack on the pass, the fencer's rear foot is brought past the front one, effectively becoming the lead foot. This movement can be used in various ways. A half-pass can be used to bring the back foot up to the lead one, after which another step can be made in any direction. A double pass is essentially two passes, moving the fencer a long way without altering the alignment of his body.

A full pass (sometimes just called a pass) reverses the feet by stepping through either forward or back. This can be done to gain distance for an attack, either directly forward or off to the side in order to void a thrust, in which case the fencer may then pass back to his normal position. Alternatively, it can be used to move from an offensive stance (with the sword arm forward) to a defensive stance (with the off hand advanced). The latter is normally used when a defensive weapon such as a dagger or buckler is used, though an unarmed off hand can defend effectively against a thrust. Some systems advocated the use of a mailed gauntlet on the off hand, which could be used to parry or grab an opponent's blade.

Using Off-Hand Weapons

Most off-hand weapons, i.e. whatever object the swordsman had in his other hand, were used primarily for defence. However, fencing with a rapier in one hand and something else in the other was significantly different to sword-only fencing; successful swordsmen understood that what they had was a weapons system consisting of two parts, much like the sword and shield. Those who learned to integrate the two weapons performed far better than those who tried to use them separately.

For example, the fencer who was used to fighting with a rapier alone might tend to make all defensive actions with the sword, forgetting that he had a dagger or buckler in the other hand. Alternatively, he might overemphasise his dagger or buckler if he was not used to having one. Both of these could lead to missed opportunities and suboptimal defence.

A well-integrated off-hand weapon was used *only* when it was the most appropriate option, and *always* when it was the most appropriate option. Thus a cut or thrust on the sword-arm side would be defended with the sword; a thrust on the off-hand side would be met with the dagger or buckler. A cut on that side might require the sword to stop it, and if so it would be used. Some defences made use of both weapons, which was excellent when done deliberately but disastrous when a panicky swordsman tried to defend with both weapons at once in an uncoordinated manner. Entanglement usually ensued even if the defence was successful – which it often was not.

Integrated use of both weapons was useful in both attack and defence. For example, a cut could be parried with the sword and then passed to the dagger, binding it out of the way while a counter was made. Most offensive actions were made with the sword, although a dagger could be highly effective at close quarters and other weapons might be useful at times.

Most of the two-weapon use portrayed in video games, like the term applied to it ('dual wielding'), is utter and probably suicidal nonsense. Trying to strike with two weapons at once was a recipe for disaster; a properly trained swordsman defended with one while he struck with the other. In this way he was properly protected against his opponent's actions and could focus on getting his own attack to the target. He might alternate between offence and defence with each weapon, but he would not commit both to the attack at once.

Various forms of off-hand dagger existed. Often referred to as a *main gauche* ('left hand' in French), the parrying dagger was quite a large, robust object that offered some form of hand protection and had a crosspiece much like a sword. A smaller knife would lack the mass necessary to parry and would require a certain amount of luck to get in the way of a blade, but might be useful for a sneaky attack at close quarters. Indeed, one function of the salute was to show that the swordsman did not have such a knife in his off hand.

The parrying dagger was capable of delivering a lethal thrust, but despite this it was very much a defensive weapon. A swordsman armed with rapier and dagger could flow between offensive and defensive stances, changing the way his weapons were presented, but his intent would always be to deliver the decisive cut or thrust with the longer and deadlier sword.

At its most basic, off-hand dagger use covered the 'inside' lines, i.e. the left side of the body for most swordsmen. An opponent's thrust could be taken well to the side and up or down, pulling his weapon much further out of position than a sword parry could ever do and leaving the sword entirely unencumbered for a return blow. It also offered a second line of defence if an opponent's blade eluded a defensive attempt with the sword, though using a dagger to parry to the 'outside' (the sword-arm side) was not an ideal situation.

The standard parrying dagger was, in many ways, a miniature sword. Specialist 'trapping' or 'sword-breaking' daggers existed, using angled quillions or a comb-like arrangement to catch and hold a blade. It is quite unlikely that a sword could be broken by such a weapon, but it might be levered out of the user's hand or bound where it was of no use for long enough to strike.

The buckler was not really a shield in the true sense. It was very small, consisting of little more than a metal rim around a cup for the hand. Passively holding a buckler in the way of an attack was not very effective; it was better thought of as a parrying weapon than a barrier. Indeed, the buckler could be used to strike to good effect. A punch with the centre of the buckler was delivered with a simple and instinctive thrusting action, while the rim could also strike using a hooking blow.

Bucklers had been in use for many decades before the Renaissance, and were well regarded for all their small size. A buckler did not get in the way of certain sword strokes in the way that a shield could, and was easy to carry hanging on the belt; this may have been the origin of the name. On the battlefield, the buckler offered only a little protection against arrows and other missiles, but it could be effective against even quite large weapons. In the early 1500s, Spanish sword and bucklermen were able to challenge pike-armed infantry by using their sword and buckler to push past the points, or diving and rolling under the pikes. Once in close, the bucklermen had the advantage over their pike-armed opponents and could set about breaking up their formations.

The cloak was more of an expedient than a weapon, though some were weaponised by having a chain running through the lower seam to weight it. A man who had the time could take off his cloak, roll it around his arm to create a padded shield, and leave the lower part hanging to entangle an attack. The main problem with this expedient was that time was not always available.

It is doubtful whether the rolled cloak could protect an arm sufficiently to block cuts without injury, though it would increase the safety with which thrusts could be set aside using the off arm. Thrusts and even cuts were better dealt with by causing them to become entangled in the dangling cloak. The ability of the hanging cloth to move would absorb much of the force of a blow – quite likely without the cloak being cut. A hanging cloak could be used to conceal the position of the swordsman's weapon.

A cloak could also be used offensively. Swept over the opponent's weapon, it could entangle and drag it aside. It might also be thrown over the opponent's head or generally in his direction as a distraction. However, it would not be wise to make too much of these tricks. A cloak was difficult to control, and a swordsman who concentrated too much on being clever with his cloak might miss an opportunity to do something more effective with his sword. He might even entangle his own weapon, leaving him highly vulnerable.

Some masters advocated the use of a pair of swords, referred to as a 'case of rapiers'. As noted above, it is probable that this was mainly a demonstration of their great skill rather than a serious fighting technique. Using two long swords at once was extremely difficult, much more so than using a long weapon and a short one. Any mistake would result in the weapons colliding or becoming entangled, rendering them temporarily useless.

As with other forms of video-game-style 'dual wielding', attacking with two rapiers at once was a recipe for disaster. A double thrust could be swept aside by a single parry; two cuts from the same side could also be stopped by a single action. An attempt to cut from both sides at once would likely be met by a thrust to the body or head. A good thrust would outreach a pair of cuts, and would likely prevent them from developing by throwing the attacker back. This was especially true for a thrust to the head, and arguably anyone attempting this sort of idiocy would deserve to be stabbed in the face.

Rather than stylish whirling and double attacks, the swordsman armed with a case of rapiers would use them carefully, one in attack and one in defence. Passes would be used to alter which side was the 'offensive' one, perhaps confounding an opponent armed with a single weapon. However, keeping both weapons in play without entangling them was a complex business, as they needed a great deal of space to move around one another.

Thus while two swords might seem to be better than one, this was not usually the case. A swordsman without the requisite level of skill, or who was made clumsy by the stress of combat, would likely either forget about one weapon and focus on the other or else make a fatal mistake that would take both out of action long enough for the opponent to strike.

A case of rapiers was better used in an exhibition bout than in a fight to the death, allowing the master to show off his skill and thus attract wealthy students and patronage. For actual combat, a parrying dagger or a buckler was a far better choice than a second rapier. It was also cheaper, easier to carry, and much quicker to deploy in an emergency. Had the case of rapiers offered sufficient advantage, its use would have been far more common despite the difficulty.

Rapiers in the New World and the Old

As noted previously, the rapier was not a battlefield weapon but a gentleman's sidearm. However, gentlemen – or at least rich and powerful men – were travelling far abroad during the Renaissance, and they took with them their rapiers. Similarly, an increasingly urbanised population in Europe created a situation where more men armed with swords were in proximity to one another than had previously been the case.

In a society where anyone with a reasonable amount of money could afford a sword and a few lessons from the local master, and anyone with pretentions of being important just had to own and display a decent sword, backstreet clashes were inevitable. Rivalries, feuds and random disagreements were settled with formal duels or impromptu brawls, possibly with multiple combatants on each side.

Most of the swordplay in such situations was likely very poor. The swordsmen involved would not, for the most part, be very well taught, experienced or used to the mortal terror of fighting against someone armed with a live weapon. They might also be drunk, and alcohol is not a performance-enhancing drug. Thus the likely situation would be a mix of opportunistic stabbings, badly misjudged and reckless attacks, desperate flailing and a great deal of posturing behind a more or less correct guard stance.

There would also be some competent swordplay, of course, but this was likely to be the exception rather than the rule. The stress of a modern sporting competition (for example, a friendly county-level foil event) can cause some quite well-trained fencers to go to pieces. Facing a real sword wielded with deadly – and perhaps even skilled – intent would be much worse, and might cause the swordsman's few lessons' worth of knowledge to evaporate.

The swordsman who had trained diligently and kept his head would have a massive advantage in such a scramble. His cautious approach would likely enable him to avoid injury until the fight was broken up or his opponent made a mistake. He might even be able to inflict a relatively minor wound, for example a tip cut along the sword arm or side of the head, and thus cause his opponent to reconsider his options. This gambit was relatively low-risk compared to attempting a killing thrust to the body or head, and might help avoid future complications arising from a dead opponent.

It should be noted that while some of the fencing masters of the era truly were masters of their art, the term could be applied to anyone who taught swordsmanship. Some of these men might not have been very good teachers; some might not have been very good swordsmen. Quite small towns might have two or more 'masters' teaching fencing; with such numbers the average quality cannot have been high.

Anyone claiming mastery was liable to be challenged by someone else who wanted to make money from sword instruction, or by the master or students of a rival school. Thus, claiming to be a fencing master might be a risky business, but it was a way for almost anyone who could afford a sword and a place to teach to make some money. Frauds, incompetents and charlatans claiming to know unstoppable secret strokes were gambling with the lives of their pupils, but it was the pupils who paid the price for this deceit.

With all of these swords on the street and men in the middle and upper classes who were willing to fight over a real or presumed slight, it is scarcely surprising that elaborate courtesy and a system of formal manners evolved. Gentlemen were advised not only on how to render courtesies to those passed in the street, but how to ensure that the recipient knew who was being bowed to. Courtesies were rendered with the precision of a sword thrust, and with similar intent – they were both a means of preventing the gentleman-swordsman from coming to harm.

Thus, armed with his good manners and his sword, the gentleman (and anyone under his protection) was well defended. His courtesies prevented other gentlemen from taking potentially lethal offence, while his rapier deterred riff-raff from trying to rob him. It was also a broad hint to others of similar station that he was offering courtesy not out of weakness but from a position of strength, and that they would be well advised to reply in kind.

The explorers, traders and conquerors who discovered areas of the world previously unknown in Europe, and then colonised, annexed or generally caused mayhem there, took with them a variety of weapons. Pikes, firearms and cannon were used against the natives of these far-off places, but expedition leaders would also be armed with rapiers or sideswords.

Thus, while the gentlemen of a Renaissance city could expect to encounter someone armed with a similar rapier, or perhaps a member of the lower orders with a club or knife, an expedition member might find himself battling all manner of strange foreign weapons. The combination of rapier, helmet and linen or metal breastplate proved effective against Aztec warriors armed with sword-clubs edged with volcanic glass, and was employed on the other side of the world against the tribesmen of South East Asia.

There is even a tale, from before the island nation closed its borders to foreigners, of merchants operating in Japan who became involved in a dispute with local samurai. Allegedly, a duel was fought, and the rapier-armed European won. However, there is no solid evidence that this occurred, and even if it did it would not be proof that one weapon is superior to another. This does not prevent the rapier-*v.*-katana debate from resurfacing every now and then.

The period just after the discovery of the 'New World', i.e. from around 1500 onwards, was also the golden age of piracy. Privateers raided the New World treasure ships, and pirates preyed on whatever vessels they encountered. Pirate havens and European colonies alike brought swords and swordsmanship from the Old World to distant places; it became possible to learn Spanish rapier technique in places as far afield as Ecuador and the Philippines.

How much influence this spread of European swordsmanship had is debatable. Those who fought against the colonists and conquerors undoubtedly studied their methods, but clashes were generally between fighting forces rather than taking the form of individual duels. Nevertheless, European swordsmanship was present and was studied in all corners of the world where Europeans settled.

The Renaissance era provides a setting for swashbuckling adventures in which the sword can play a vital role. Later eras have an inconvenient number of effective firearms available, but the Renaissance setting allows for dramatic sword fights for precisely the same reason swords were carried – guns were not really viable as a means of personal protection. Thus d'Artagnan and his comrades from the King's Musketeers, ostensibly soldiers whose primary weapon is a musket, do most of their battling with swords.

Dumas set his novel *The Three Musketeers* in 1625, at a time when the heavy rapier was soon to be supplanted by smaller, lighter versions that would eventually become the small-sword. Portrayals of swordplay in the endless series of Musketeer movies tend to be inaccurate or anachronistic, often depicting very light swords that were not in use at the time making fast actions that would not be possible with a rapier.

However, within a few years the 'late rapier period' would begin, and from around 1650 to 1680 a family of smaller and lighter transition rapiers would emerge, finally leading to a very different style of fencing made possible by a light and relatively short sword, the small-sword.

CHAPTER 6

A Gentleman's Companion: The Small-Sword

From the mid-1600s onward, the rapier began to fall out of fashion. For all its effectiveness in combat, it was a large piece of metal to carry around all day. Its hilt chafed clothing, which was a serious problem in an era in which a gentleman would have at best only a few outfits and when threadbare clothes would attract derision. The rapier was also not well suited to use in crowded streets. It was slow to draw and, while rabid critics such as George Silver may have overstated its slowness on the defensive, it was indeed better suited to offence than defence.

A series of what modern historians call 'transition rapiers' began to appear, with lighter and shorter blades than their predecessors. These weapons could move more quickly and were easier to use in confined spaces. They were also less tiring to fence with and less cumbersome to carry. A thrust with one of these weapons was potentially as lethal as that of a heavy rapier, though the wound track was narrower.

The transition rapier and the small-sword that evolved from it were not any more effective in combat than the previous designs, but they did offer advantages of their own to the swordsman who knew how to make use of them. That is to say: the rapier was not swept aside by a new wave of much better swords – its eclipse was more due to social changes – but the new generation of swords would not have caught on if they were greatly inferior to the mid-Renaissance rapier.

A New Style of Fencing

Among the transition weapons that emerged in the late seventeenth century was the colichemarde. This had a wide blade close to the hilt, narrowing sharply towards the point. In this way it balanced strength for the parry with lightness of tip for fast actions. It was well suited to a fencing style based on parrying with the sword and then riposting rather than using the off hand for defence or counter-attacking with opposition.

This marked the beginning of a transition from a generally single-tempo style of fencing, in which a thrust was ideally met with a counterstroke in opposition – i.e. attack and defence were made in the same action – to a two-tempi style. The colichemarde moved fast enough that the swordsman could parry then counter and still have a good chance to hit. Trying this with a heavy rapier could often give the opponent the opportunity to retire out of reach.

The new style of parry-riposte was often used with little in the way of body mechanics, as the sword was now light enough to be moved with just the arm. This marked a fundamental change in the way fencers fought. It was not necessarily superior as such, but it was better suited to the weapons in use at the time. One of the key advantages to parrying in this manner was the ability to make successive or compound parries. With a counter-attack in opposition, if the swordsman misjudged his action he would be hit whether or not his counter landed, whereas a failed parry could be followed with another until the opponent's blade was found and deflected.

The riposte that followed a successful parry was made in the same manner as an attack – usually but not always in opposition – to hold the opponent's blade clear and prevent any remise of the attack from being successful. Where a counter-attack had to be committed to as soon as the opponent began his attack, the intent to parry-riposte could be broken down into its constituent actions. A riposte could be made instantly, or the fencer could feint his riposte in the hope that the opponent would commit to a parry. If the opponent took the bait, the swordsman could then deceive the parry by attacking in a different line. Alternatively, the fencer could parry and then choose not to riposte if the situation looked a little risky.

This increase in the number of options came at the same time as blades were moving faster, arguably making an encounter far more dangerous.

A swordsman could land a telling blow more or less by accident; a good fencer might need to be more wary of a very poor opponent than one who was just slightly inferior to him. Unpredictability due to incompetence, combined with a fast blade, could be dangerous to all concerned.

A properly trained opponent would react predictably to what the swordsman did. This created the opportunity to outwit him by making him react to one action, creating a vulnerability that the swordsman would be able to exploit. An unskilled fencer might not see the feint or the opportunity left dangling in front of him, or might panic and thrust blindly when a more skilled opponent would be busy parrying and thus not likely to impale the unfortunate swordsman who had done (almost) everything right.

It thus became more important than ever to fence safely, which meant that the swordsman must only commit to an action when it had a good chance of success and when there was little risk of being hit in return – whether through the opponent's good fencing or bad. One way to achieve this was to control the opponent's blade by attacks upon it, for example beating it aside, or taking the blade with a bind. Simply grabbing the opponent's blade was always an option, though this was a better idea if it had no cutting edge.

Another way to create a safe opening was to use a parry and riposte. It was much easier to hit an opponent who had committed to an attack and advanced into range than one who stood ready to defend himself, but obviously a prerequisite for the successful riposte was a parry that defeated the opponent's attack while maintaining good control of the swordsman's own blade.

A key principle underlying the successful parry was the 'principle of defence', which states that defensive actions should be made by opposing them with the forte, the strong part of the blade close to the hand guard. This was not just about blade strength; a swordsman who received a blow further along the blade could find his weapon knocked aside or even out of his hand. Parries were generally made with the true edge, but false-edge parries could be effective against the thrusts of light blades.

Tactically, it was advantageous to parry as late as possible. This denied the opponent the chance to slip around, or deceive, the parry, and ensured that he was heavily committed at the moment he found that his attack had failed. A late parry offered the greatest chance of a successful riposte – but being a fraction too late could have quite serious consequences.

Parrying close to the hilt fulfilled all of these principles – lateness, correct alignment of the hand and using the strongest part of the blade.

The colichemarde became obsolete as the move towards lighter weapons continued. Its thick forte gave it strength that was not needed when parrying a small-sword or similar light blade, and added weight that slowed the colichemarde down unnecessarily. Its popularity waned in the early 1700s until it was fully supplanted by the small-sword.

The Small-Sword

The small-sword was not a single design of weapon but a family of generally similar weapons all known by the same name, or rather names. Small-swords are variously referred to as walking swords, court swords or town swords. Sometimes these terms are used specifically for a given weapon, but often the entire family of small-swords is referred to by a generic title.

In general terms, the small-sword was a light thrusting sword, usually with no cutting edge and a blade in the 80- to 85-cm range. It had a fairly small hand guard and a knuckle bow, and vestigial quillions at most. The ricasso of the rapier survived in the form of the pas d'ane, which might include rings that seem to invite a finger to be slipped through them. In fact, this was not done.

Most small-sword fencing systems specified one of two ways for the sword to be held: either a 'sabre grip' with the thumb along the back of the handle or a 'pinch grip' where the first finger and thumb held the pas d'ane and the other fingers curled gently around the handle. In both methods, the weapon was held fairly lightly and a certain amount of shifting of grip could be used to facilitate various actions.

Examples of small-sword design varied from what were essentially light rapiers to predecessors of the modern fencing foil. Indeed, the foil was invented as a training tool for the small-sword, and derived much of its original body of technique from the small-sword.

The classical foil technique taught in modern Olympic-style fencing classes is in most ways closely similar to – though in some instances it is also very different from – small-sword technique. The competition-specific material that overlays this body of technique has little to do with the small-sword; the sport of fencing has evolved greatly since its roots as a training exercise for the duel or self-defence.

Some variances in small-sword design were imposed by fashion, some by practicality and some by changes in the environment in which the weapon was used from the late seventeenth century onwards. The spadroon, a very similar weapon to the small-sword, was developed for military use. It possessed a slightly broader blade with two cutting edges, and indeed was sometimes referred to as 'the cutting sword' to differentiate it from other small-sword types.

Spadroon technique included cuts, which were of no interest to a small-sword fencer whose weapon could not make them. Both bodies of technique of course included defences against cuts, since a small-swordsman might well come up against a spadroon or one of the heavier cutting swords that existed during its long career, such as a backsword or a military sabre.

Small-sword fencing evolved over a long period, developing from the strokes of the transition rapier and the colichemarde into a number of small-sword-specific systems. Many early small-sword masters were rapier instructors adapting to the new weapon, while later masters were operating in an era of repeating firearms, where the sword was a sporting tool as much as a weapon for combat.

Like the rapier before it, the small-sword was carried as a sidearm by gentlemen and military officers, and was used for duelling and self-defence. Most swordsmen would choose to arm themselves with something more robust if battle threatened, but the small-sword could and did serve well at need. It became the standard duelling sword in much of Europe, although conventions about what was permitted in a duel and how it was to be conducted did vary according to time and place.

The off hand could be used to defend against a thrust under most circumstances, although some duelling systems forbade this. In general, however, the sword was used for both attack and defence, with the body often sharply bladed (turned sideways) to present a smaller target. This took advantage of the weapon's speed and lightness; those parts of the body not necessary to its use were kept as far out of harm's way as possible.

Notably, in many systems the off hand was raised behind the fencer and used as a counterbalance for movement in much the same manner as a cat's tail. The arm was dropped when lunging and raised again when recovering from the lunge, assisting with balance in both a physiological and psychological manner. This largely applied to formal fencing and training, or a duelling convention in which the use of the off hand was forbidden. In a street brawl, use of the off hand for defence was, like any other expedient, perfectly acceptable.

The small-sword was a highly lethal implement in skilled hands. As a thrusting weapon, it delivered penetrating attacks, which were potentially fatal anywhere on the torso, providing the weapon penetrated to a depth of 5 cm or more. Thrusts to some other parts of the body could also be directly fatal if they penetrated an artery or critical organ.

However, lethality was not the same thing as what, in the world of firearms, is known as 'stopping power'. A small-sword thrust might not immediately stop the opponent from acting, and whether the opponent collapsed three seconds after being hit, or died of wound infection three weeks later, mattered not at all to the fencer who made an unwary thrust and was fatally hit in return. Thus all attacks had to be made on the assumption that they would not stop the opponent from acting, and were delivered in a manner such as not to expose the fencer to a return blow.

In general, two kinds of attack could be delivered: weakening and finishing. A weakening attack would not put the opponent out of the fight but did reduce his ability to fight on, and could perhaps provoke a surrender or expeditious retreat. Thrusts to the limbs, as well as most strikes with the pommel, were weakening attacks. The small-sword did not have the ability to make opportunistic tip cuts as the rapier could, but the user did have a choice between relatively low-risk thrusts to the opponent's sword arm and lead leg or an attempt to finish him with a deep thrust to the neck or torso.

Instantly fatal thrusts were hard to accomplish, but an action that caused the opponent to collapse after a few seconds was still a finishing blow. However, attempting to deliver such a thrust was risky, as it meant coming within reach of the opponent's weapon while making a very committed attack. Most masters advocated deep attacks to the body only for 'salle play', i.e. training and practice within the fencing salle (training room).

For a serious fight, it was generally considered advisable to make one or more weakening attacks and then seek a finish when the opponent was made vulnerable, assuming of course that he did not flee or surrender when wounded.

Small-sword systems varied somewhat, but in general there were considered to be four orthodox lines of attack, divided high/low and inside/outside. Exactly which line an attack followed was defined not by the target point so much as by the path of the attack relative to the opponent's sword arm.

The distinction between high and low lines is fairly obvious. The line of the sternum and bottom ribs was generally considered to separate high and low lines. An attack to the head, sword arm or upper chest was 'in the high line'; the abdomen, flanks and legs fell in the low line. However, the path to the target from the fencer's sword arm was an important consideration; a downward thrust into the low line made from a very high hand position would be defended differently from one originating from a low position.

The concept of inside and outside was also fairly straightforward. The 'outside' was the side on which the fencer held his sword, usually the right. Inside was the other side. However, again the point of origin of an attack was highly relevant. An attack to the outside lines that originated from a point further to the defender's sword-arm side than his weapon was currently situated could be parried by moving the blade outwards. An attack on the same spot on the target made from 'inside' the opponent's blade required a different defence.

The target was thus divided into four general zones: high outside was the easiest to reach for the opponent, low inside was much farther away if both fencers stood in an orthodox guard position. Low outside and high inside fell somewhere in between. One consequence of this was that a parry that carried a thrust to the inside had more time to be completed, as that side of the fencer's body was angled away from the attack. Conversely, parrying to the outside had the advantage that the fencer could advance 'past the point', closer to the opponent than his sword point, and make it very difficult to bring the weapon back on line in time to pose a threat.

Most systems taught fencers to begin with their blades engaged in the line of Tierce or Quarte. 'Engaged' in this case meant that they were positioned such that the opponent could not thrust directly and hit the swordsman; his blade must be cleared or evaded first. A guard in Tierce covered the high outside line; Quarte covered the high inside line. These two positions formed the basis of most small-sword fencing systems as they covered the most likely lines of attack.

If a swordsman were engaged with an opponent in Tierce and moved his blade around the opposing one, he would be moving into what was termed an open line. The opponent could close this line, for example by moving his weapon laterally across to Quarte or in a circular manner to resume the engagement in Tierce. If this were done while an attack was being made, a parry would result; if the opponent were seeking an opening but not actively attacking, it would be termed a change of engagement.

The same movements used to parry were used to change the engagement. Small-sword bouts were characterised by many changes of engagement and other preparations, such as beats on the blade. Both fencers would be seeking to either get into an open line or force the opponent to follow, hoping that he made a mistake that could be exploited. There was nothing new about this concept of course, but it was critical to small-sword play and affected all aspects of how the weapon was used.

The ideal of the small-sword bout was that there would only be one thrust. A perhaps lengthy period of preparation would eventually result in one fencer winning the line and having a clear shot. The reality tended to be a lot scrappier, but all fencers were taught never to commit to an offensive action (including a riposte) unless they had a good chance of hitting and little of being struck in return.

Attacking into a closed or closing line was pointless, and could result in being hit on the riposte. Instead, all efforts were bent towards either finding an open line or, better, manipulating the opponent into opening a line just as the fencer attacked into it. Good small-sword fencers were cautious fellows, who preferred not to trust to reflexes and the speed of their admittedly fast weapons. Instead they worked to set up an opponent, to make certain of his vulnerability, and only then committed themselves to strike.

Attacks and ripostes were, almost exclusively, made 'in tempo' or 'in time', i.e. at a time when the opponent was not attacking. The small-sword's characteristics were best suited to use as a two-tempi weapon, i.e. normally a fencer would parry then riposte rather than attempting to land a stop hit with or without opposition. Such 'contratempo' actions were sometimes used, however, generally in conjunction with an evasion such as a void or leg slip.

As a general rule, contratempo or counteroffensive actions would constitute extremely bad fencing unless accompanied by a defensive action. Counter-attacking in the hope that the opponent would miss, or sticking a thrust out in a panic whenever threatened, was the hallmark of the nervous incompetent, and would annoy other fencers in the salle. In an encounter with sharps it was a virtual guarantee that the fencer would be wounded or killed.

The exception to this rule was when the fencer used a void to protect himself. A void could be used alone, but this would hardly advance the fencer's cause. He might use a desperate dodge or leap backwards to escape being skewered, but this was a temporary expedient that must be followed by further actions to prevent the opponent from pressing forward while the fencer was out of position from his void.

Perhaps the commonest void, and certainly the most mundane, was the leg slip. This was nothing more than moving the lead leg back to avoid an attack aimed at it. This could be performed as a pass, transferring the fencer's weight backwards, or as a short slip followed by a return to the same position. The latter could be riskier – the fencer might not move his leg far enough, or might find himself returning forward towards a point aimed at his face. It did, however, preserve measure and thus give the best chance of a successful counter-attack.

Similarly, it was possible to void an attack to the head or upper body by leaning back, though this could unbalance the fencer, or twisting out of the way of a thrust. These movements might make a counter-attack difficult or cause a loss of equilibrium, and in any case might not be enough to avoid the attack. The use of a volte or demi-volte was a more certain defence.

The volte was an evasive action in which the fencer moved his rear foot around behind his front in such a way that his body pivoted out of the way of a thrust. In the demi-volte, the fencer pivoted about 90°; a full volte turned him almost completely around to face away from his opponent. Timing was everything in this movement. Since it moved the off-hand side of the fencer's body a long way off the line and the sword-arm side hardly at all, it was primarily efficacious against a thrust to the inside lines.

The accompanying counter-attack was made by presenting the point for the opponent to run on to. The point must remain steady as the fencer pivoted, so he was required to turn his head and continue looking at the opponent as the body turned away. Performed correctly at the right time, the volte or demi-volte was an extremely effective and dramatic action. It was considered too risky for serious combat by many masters, however.

As an alternative to voiding, the swordsman could use a stop-thrust to prevent his opponent from attacking. A stop-thrust was normally directed at the sword arm, though a robust attack to the face might well serve the same function. A stop-thrust was more than a counter-attack; it had to stop the opponent's attack as well as wound him. Thus it had to strike cleanly and in an area that would halt the opponent's stroke – a successful counter-thrust was little use to the swordsman who was killed at the same time.

A stop-thrust could be made in the absence of a blade, i.e. without opposing the opponent's thrust, only if the fencer were convinced it would stop the attack. The usual method was to attempt to pin the fencer's bicep to his body as his arm extended or to thrust into the forearm. Alternatively, a stop-thrust could be made in opposition, as was common in the rapier fencing systems that the small-sword displaced.

The Development of Small-Sword Fencing

In most small-sword systems, thrusts were made at head height with the point angled down, enabling the swordsman's arm to provide some protection for his face and head. The principle of true and false edges was followed, even though the weapon usually had no cutting edge, as this aligned the hand well for both attack and defence. Most parries were made with the true edge, as were beats on the opponent's blade, though the false edge could be used against a thrust. A cut must be parried with the true edge; to do otherwise was to risk having the weapon knocked from the swordsman's hand.

In general, most small-sword systems used a fairly upright position, with the weight more heavily on the back foot than the front and the head leaning back a little for protection. This position had the effect of slowing forward movement but facilitating a rapid retreat, which was thought desirable by many masters. One of the earliest great small-sword instructors, a Frenchman named André de Liancour, advocated a stance with the weight heavily on the back foot, making it difficult to advance boldly.

This might have been purely because de Liancour thought this was the best way to fence, or at least in part because his students included members of the French court. A style that made it hard to rush hot-headedly on to an opponent's point and easy to fly out of range if threatened helped ensure that de Liancour's students did not get themselves killed in a manner that could be blamed on him.

De Liancour published a manual of fence in 1686 that set forth his system and illustrated it in the most remarkable manner. De Liancour's fencers demonstrate the movements and postures of his system against the backdrop of land and naval warfare, and other highly complex illustrations that can distract the reader from the information being presented.

De Liancour's system is the earliest to make no mention of cutting actions. He does take pains to advocate treating a fencing lesson as a matter of life and death rather than sport, by which he presumably means recreation. It may be that many of his pupils were wont to regard sword instruction as a pastime or distraction rather than preparation to defend their lives. De Liancour did not approve of this attitude and strove to make his pupils understand the importance of what he was trying to impart to them.

De Liancour and other small-sword masters presented certain basic principles that underlie small-sword fencing. Stance, body positioning and footwork were absolutely essential and fundamental. A problem here would ripple through everything the fencer did, and would not be offset by skilled bladework alone. Similarly, proper attention must be paid to line. Attacks, parries and other actions should be made in the correct line with the appropriate orientation of hand and arm to give protection and cover when attacking or riposting.

The speed with which a small-sword can move made this last an extremely important consideration. If a fencer was lazy about taking and holding the line while he made his riposte (i.e. he failed to keep his weapon in a position to stop his opponent from thrusting again) then he ran the risk of being hit by a remise. There was no guarantee that the opponent would not simply poke again after being parried; the swordsman had to safeguard himself against bad fencing as well as good.

In the event that the line was not taken and held, the riposte would probably land with much greater penetration than a parried thrust that was replaced on target and pushed in – but that did not make a 'double hit' of this sort desirable. The only ways to ensure it did not happen were to riposte in opposition, holding the line closed, or to strike while the opponent's blade was moving in a 'safe' direction.

It was safe to thrust in the absence of a blade, i.e. where the weapons are not in opposition, when the opponent's sword was moving or facing in a direction where it did not threaten the fencer and could not quickly begin to do so. An opponent whose sloppy fencing had taken his point off line, or who had momentarily lost control of his sword after a collision of blades, could safely be attacked in absence of blade. Indeed, it might be necessary if his blade were not available to be opposed.

The small-sword masters also advocated that attention should be paid to measure, i.e. the distance between the fencers. Differences in height and reach might require measure to be re-evaluated; proper measure was not a fixed distance. A swordsman had to be aware of what his opponent could do at a given distance and of what he himself could do; it might be that the opponent could reach with a simple thrust across a distance that would require the swordsman to make a pass or lunge. Mistakenly believing himself far enough away from the opponent to have time to react would in fact place this fencer in mortal danger.

Small-sword fencing, no matter what the system, was made up of a relatively small number of movements, some of which could be used in various ways or for different purposes. For example, a circular movement of the blade could be used as a parry, taking the swordsman's blade inside that of the opponent and carrying it off the line of attack, or could be used to defeat a lateral parry by going around it to find an open line.

Small-sword parries fell into three categories: simple (or lateral), circular and semicircular. A lateral parry moved the swordsman's blade across his body to push aside a thrust. As with all thrusting weapons, the point had to be kept in line with the opponent, so the parry was a movement of the hand and hilt, maintaining the alignment of the point at the opponent, rather than a pivoting action that would move the point far off line. The hilt and forte of the blade had to move into the line to be 'closed', after which the point was already aligned and could be pushed forward to make a riposte.

A circular parry (known as a counter-parry or contre-parry) moved the blade in a circle, bringing it quickly inside the opponent's thrust and pushing it off line. This required minimal movement, and a semicircular parry needed scarcely more. The latter was normally used to defend against a thrust that was aimed at a higher or lower target than the swordsman's hand.

Although fencers were trained to make multiple attacks and parries, this did not occur very often outside the training environment. Most fencing bouts or actual fights would take the form of one or more 'phrases', or sequences of actions, with distinct breaks between them. Usually there would be a period of manoeuvring, some preparation, and an attempt to hit. If this were not successful then it might be followed by one or more parries and ripostes, which might or might not result in a hit. The fencers might also close and seize or grapple, perhaps attempting a disarm, but commonly they would move apart after an inconclusive exchange and begin a new phrase with renewed attempts to win an advantage.

The longer a phrase went on for, the more messy it was likely to become, which increased the risk of being hit by accident. The small-sword masters knew that in any phrase that went beyond the first attempt to hit, the fencer who best retained control of his emotions, his body position and his weapon would likely emerge victorious.

The answer of course was to open distance as soon as the fencer felt he was no longer in control of the phrase. If the opponent were under pressure and becoming sloppy, pressing the attack might be a good option, but once control was lost it was best to re-establish it by breaking off and resetting. A rapid retirement, perhaps using one or more passes, was advisable at this point. Under de Liancour's system, the fencer was primed to do exactly that.

Although France had not been very influential in the rapier era, small-sword fencing quickly came to dominate in the French school of thinking. This was perhaps due to the pattern of adoption of the small-sword; conversion to the new weapon started earlier in France than in many other places so it was perhaps inevitable that others would follow French thinking rather than starting again from first principles.

Given the close relations between France and Scotland, it is not surprising that the small-sword systems being developed in France were of great interest to Scotsmen too. Among them was Sir William Hope, who published his first manual of fence in 1687. It is perhaps indicative of how the small-sword was developing that Hope later decided that his system as put forth in *The Scots Fencing Master* was suboptimal, and revised his thinking considerably.

Hope's later work is particularly interesting in that he draws a huge distinction between the formal technique of the fencing salle and the life-or-death scramble of a street fight. In Hope's time, fencing was an essential skill for a young gentleman to learn, especially if he had come into money from industry rather than inheriting it. The ability to engage in beautiful 'salle play' was a way of showing off the swordsman's culture and refinement, and was important to his social advancement.

However, Hope's advice to the swordsman suddenly confronted with a live blade outside a tavern in Leith was to eschew all that beautiful technique in favour of a simple set of highly effective options. To a great extent this came down to using circular motions to carry the opponent's blade to the outside (in Tierce) and then run him through.

Hope then went on to publish (in 1707) his highly influential *New, Short and Easy Method*, by which time his thinking had again developed. Within the new method, Hope attempted to encapsulate all the principles of swordplay with any weapon, be it a small-sword or a cutting weapon like the broadsword or backsword. This search for a scientific 'universal theory of all swordplay' was indicative of the thinking of the day.

Hope was particularly concerned with avoiding a contretemps, by which he meant an attack made as the opponent was also doing so. A skilled fencer might be able to use opposition of the blade to do this without being hit, but Hope still recommended against it. Instead he advocated ways of making the swordsman very hard to hit, enabling him to wait for or perhaps force an opening against a frustrated opponent.

Much use was made of the off hand and a 'hanging' guard position, in which the hilt was held high and the blade angled down. This was borrowed from the backsword, a heavy-bladed cutting weapon that impressed Hope, and although not by any means unknown in other systems, its emphasis was unusual.

Hope also advocated that the lunge be short, which was possibly due to a combination of the bad footing found in most places that swordsmen might go and the nature of the footwear of the day, which was not well suited to a deep lunge. Lunges had become popular during the mid- to late rapier period, but Hope and other small-sword masters considered that they must be regarded with caution.

One concept that all small-sword masters agreed on was that the lunge was not used to move from place to place, but to deliver an attack on the target. It was not an attack in itself (indeed, a lunge without a blade action could be considered a form of assisted suicide), but acted as a vehicle to carry the attack to the target. Attacks, in short, were to be made with the weapon and not with footwork.

To lunge with a small-sword or most other weapons, the fencer carried out whatever preparatory action seemed desirable (e.g. a beat to knock aside the opponent's weapon) and made a thrust by extending the arm. If the thrust did not suffice to reach the target, then a lunge (or alternatively a step or a pass) was made to cover the necessary distance. In order to keep the fencer's body as far away from the opponent as possible, the lunge was only begun once the blade action was well developed.

To deliver the lunge, the fencer's front foot was lifted, and he pushed himself forward using his rear foot. A common fault among fencers of all eras was to treat the lunge as a big step or to throw the fencer's head and shoulders forward. This led to bad body structure and a slow, coasting lunge that could be badly overcommitted. Instead, the lunge was driven by the back foot and accelerated all the way to the target. Ideally the front foot should land as the point entered the target with the foot coming down heel first and rolling flat. Momentum was absorbed by flexing the front leg, and of course by the resilience of the target's flesh.

In 1763, Domenico Angelo published what is today the best known of all small-sword manuals, *The School of Fencing*. In it, he advocates that lunges need not be hugely deep and long. Angelo recommended a distance of a foot's length, or two at most. The head should be up and the back straight at the end of the lunge, and the front knee should not describe an angle greater than 90°. The knee of the front leg should be over the foot, not forward or to the side. These principles are still used in the modern sporting lunge, though the latter is often very deep and overlong by small-sword fencing standards.

The unarmed hand and arm were used as a counterbalance during the lunge, straightening out backwards as the lunge developed. Angelo advocated lowering the arm position to just above and parallel to the rear thigh; some other masters preferred to keep it straight out backwards. Most suggest that the hands should be in the same alignment – a pronated sword hand should be matched by a pronated rear hand, and so forth.

To recover from the lunge, normally the fencer would move backward, his rear foot remaining in place and the front leg pushing him back in a reverse lunge to finish in a normal guard stance. Recovery forward was also possible by means of bringing forward the back foot to resume a normal position, though this tends to result in a naturally lower stance. The rear arm was brought back up to its normal position to assist recovery; some masters advocated continuing this movement to bring the arm forward as an additional defence while recovering, and then returning it to its rearward position.

Angelo's system can be considered representative of 'vanilla flavour' small-sword fencing. It was formulated at a time when the art had matured from an adapted rapier system to a fighting style in its own right. Angelo's positions and actions are, for the most part, familiar to the modern foil or épée fencer, largely because these systems developed out of mature small-sword fencing and use a weapon that, although much lighter, is broadly similar in terms of its length, mode of use and usual reliance on two-tempi actions.

Angelo's system is often regarded as one of the main influences in converting fencing into a sporting activity. However, the mid- to late eighteenth century was a time when the sword was an essential self-defence weapon. Other sword masters were still publishing books on the use of the small-sword in combat a century after Angelo's work was published. Some of these manuals were civilian in nature, dealing with small-sword play for social, duelling and recreational purposes. Others were military and covered the instruction with the sword that an officer should receive.

Military sword instruction would usually include advice on how to fight against various other weapons, ranging from cutting swords to pikes and even pistols. The small-sword was the standard dress weapon and officer's badge of rank until the abandonment of swords in combat, so even after revolvers had become the practical option it was still necessary to maintain a system of sword instruction as part of military training.

The Small-Sword in Combat

Against another small-sword or a similar weapon, the small-sword could be used in a fairly delicate and subtle manner. An elegant exchange of parries and ripostes might follow a period of searching for an opening. This was not really possible when the small-sword met a different weapon; any combat between mismatched weapons tends to be short.

For the military or naval officer, the small-sword was a badge of rank that might be useful in an emergency but would likely be put aside if battle threatened. A naval officer would likely take a brutally simple cutlass into a boarding action if he had the choice. An army officer might engage an enemy officer armed similarly to himself, but was just as likely to use a pistol or not engage at all – his job was to direct the complex machine that was an infantry company or larger formation, and not to heroically attack the foe with his sword.

Thus the most likely situation where the small-sword would see use was a formally arranged duel or perhaps an unscheduled encounter in the streets. The small-swordist might be outnumbered in such a fight, but it was still personal combat rather than a battlefield action.

The small-swordist had certain advantages that were given to him by his weapon. It was fast, precise and lethal, with enough reach to be effective without being awkward in a narrow street. It could parry most weapons if used correctly, and if it would not be able to push aside a heavier sword then it could often slip past. It was also more reliable than the pistols of the day, which might well fail to fire altogether and, once discharged, were useful only as clubs.

On the other hand, the small-swordist had to be adept at getting his point aimed at the opponent, which was a problem if he had a close-quarters weapon such as a knife or a belaying pin and was determined to close distance. Once past the point the opponent was safe from a thrust unless the small-swordsman could bring his arm back far enough to get the point into play. He could not make an opportunistic cut, but since there was no way for an opponent to be certain whether his sword actually had an edge, he might be able to fool those around him into being respectful of the possibility.

The small-sword also lacked stopping power. Where a big, graphic slash might be actually less lethal than a thrust into the lung, the small-swordsman could not rely on his opponent collapsing straight away even if such a thrust were delivered. His general strategy had to be one of finding an opportunity to thrust deep into the opponent then quickly retreat, after which the small-swordsman had to stay alive until his opponent's lung filled up with blood or other effects of a thrust took hold.

Against a weapon like a knife, the swordsman's best defence was deterrence. A point held in line, i.e. threatening the opponent, could be used to keep him at bay. The knifeman might try to swat aside the small-sword, but it could move fast enough to evade such an attempt and remain a threat. If the opportunity presented itself the swordsman could deliver a quick thrust, but he was well advised to be wary of having his blade seized or getting it caught in the opponent's flesh.

An overzealous attack, or a situation where an unwary enemy rushed on to the point, could be disastrous. The slenderness of the small-sword meant that an opponent might be impaled quite far up the blade, perhaps getting close enough to stab or slash with his knife before collapse occurred. The swordsman then had the choice of trying to prevent this, for example by grappling the knife hand, or letting go of his weapon and staying out of reach until the attacker fell down.

Grappling and wrestling were a highly useful adjunct to swordsmanship for this sort of situation. An opponent could be kicked, or struck with the pommel of the sword, as well as being tripped or thrown. Grappling could also be used for what modern combat instructors call weapon retention, enabling the swordsman to prevent his weapon from being snatched from his grasp or immobilised. Overall, however, the best defence was to use the mobility of the swordsman and his fast weapon to confound all attempts to get past it, and to wait for a chance to thrust.

The small-sword was in use for such a long time that its user might encounter a backsword or similar heavy cutting sword, or the sabre that occupied the same niche in later years. The backswordist or sabreur was at a disadvantage in terms of speed, but his weapon would knock a small-sword aside on a solid contact, and could snap it if a solid connection were made.

The small-swordsman could successfully parry a heavier weapon, providing he observed the principle of defence, i.e. the blow was taken at the strongest part of the blade, near the hilt. Allowing a backsword to smash into the middle of his blade might deprive the small-swordsman of about half of it, so precision was of paramount importance on the defensive.

One gambit put forward by certain small-sword masters was to keep the sword out of harm's way, for example by angling it back over the shoulder, and to tempt the opponent into a committed strike with his heavier sword. This could be done by leaning forward a little, offering the head as a target. When the bait was taken, the small-swordsman could sway back to let the cutting sword go past his face, then deliver a thrust into the lung. He would then have to retire smartly to avoid a follow-up blow, relying on the speed of his weapon to get it out of the way before the opponent struck a second time.

Obviously such a gambit was highly risky, but there were few other options besides exploiting the relative slowness of the opponent's weapon by tempting him to commit himself unwisely. Taking the offensive was hazardous; if the opponent made a parry it could likely be deceived by the faster small-sword, but there was no guarantee that the opponent's riposte by cut would not be launched, whether the blades met or not. If so, the small-swordsman might impale his opponent and then be dreadfully hacked for his trouble. If the blades met, his lighter sword would be knocked aside and he would be unable to defend against the riposte.

As a general rule, a fencer armed with a heavier sword would want blade contact while the swordsman with a lighter weapon would tend to avoid it. His small-sword could make quick movements that threatened the opponent and then evaded his response, ideally forcing him to move his heavier sword around. This was not only tiring but also tended to result in ever larger movements; any action with a heavy blade was inevitably more committed than one made with a very light sword. The small-swordist's best option was to draw the opponent into making repeated movements until a gap opened up, then thrust through it before the opponent could react.

The modern Historical Fencing calendar includes 'duelling weapons' tournaments, in which the use of small-swords, spadroons, military sabres and duelling sabres are all allowed. Each has its own characteristics, though the small-sword and spadroon differ to only a small degree. The author's observation of and participation in several bouts have led to the opinion that, on the whole, the sabre fencer seems to have the advantage. However, this may be misleading. For one thing, the selection of fencers may have matched differing levels of skill against one another; the sample was not large enough to create a reasonable average.

More importantly, perhaps, the small-swordists may not have been trained to deal with cutting weapons, whereas the sabreurs have wider experience. The sabre can thrust, although this is a secondary mode of use, and so a properly trained sabreur is used to receiving thrusts and dealing with them. Our own research has shown that the small-sword can parry a sabre cut and can riposte fast enough to land a telling hit without being cut. This, however, requires a steady nerve and a high level of skill, so perhaps the only conclusion that can be drawn is that the fencer who best uses the advantages offered by his weapon will win.

The Curious Custom of the Duel

The problem of mismatched weapons rarely occurred in a duel situation. Standard weapons for duelling were prescribed throughout much of Europe, and even when duelling was forbidden by law there were still rules that had to be followed.

Duelling held the curious position of being socially acceptable yet illegal in many areas, and often the unspoken custom was that so long as the affair was conducted properly and nobody died, no serious investigation would be made. Participants and onlookers would not give evidence, or would politely evade questions, and the matter would be allowed to drop.

A death required investigation, and was usually considered to be murder. Thus a duellist might win his affair of honour and then be condemned to the gallows. However, he did have one last chance. At his trial, the jury might acquit him despite the certainty of guilt. This would occur if the jurors felt that they were not willing to sentence a man to death for doing something as socially acceptable as fighting for honour. Some high-ranking officials and even royalty agreed with this sentiment, and would write pardons for prospective duellists, which were carried throughout and after the proceedings.

All this made the law on duelling very difficult to enforce, providing that the affair was conducted properly according to the customs of the time. The formality of the occasion made acceptable what would otherwise be a rather unpleasant attempt at mutual murder, and ensured that allegations of unfair play and the like could not be levelled at either participant.

Duelling was nothing new; the Norsemen had customs for an agreed encounter, which might require matched weapons and a formal set of rules (a Holmgang duel) or an anything-goes challenge fight (an Einvigi duel). In the Middle Ages the judicial duel was used to determine guilt on the assumption that God would grant victory to whoever was in the right.

The judicial duel was a legal matter used to settle a dispute, and was subject to various rules. Some of these were quite bizarre, such as how a husband and wife were to fight in a manner that was fair to both. This involved the man standing in a hole and armed with a club; the woman was free to move and armed with a rock inside a sling made of cloth. According to Hans Talhoffer's 1467 *Fechtbuch*, this sort of affair often involved attempts at strangling one another as well as striking blows.

The later duel moved away from such odd concepts and attempted to ensure fairness by matching the weapons of the combatants and choosing ground that gave neither an advantage. Rules might allow for the use of the off hand, or not, and might not permit grappling. Care was also taken to ensure that neither duellist wore armour or other protection concealed under his clothing or brought additional weapons.

The duel was a curious situation in which a man was expected to fight but could be executed for winning. He could not refuse to fight – society of the time would spurn a gentleman who did so – and under many circumstances was expected to issue a challenge even if he did not wish to do so. His reputation would be ruined, his business impossible to conduct, if he did not follow the duelling custom that, illegal as it might be, was expected of him.

The duel was not really about who was right and who was wrong. It had no legal value in the manner of a judicial duel. It was purely about defending honour in the sense of challenging those who slighted the gentleman or otherwise offended him. This could lead to meaningless fights over trivialities, but it did reduce the number of violent incidents erupting at random in the streets.

By formalising the duel, society created a safety valve for outrage and also a system whereby transgressions against the accepted social order could be punished. Society was effectively enforcing the values that suited its members by this unofficial but very effective means. The best way to avoid a duel was to be exquisitely courteous, deferential to those who had power or wealth, and to take care to be seen to be honest in one's dealings.

This included payment of debts incurred in ridiculously high-stakes card games, ensuring that promises were fully understood by all parties and then seen to be kept, and otherwise behaving in an outwardly gentlemanly manner. Cheating, lying and stealing were among the many vices of the eighteenth- or nineteenth-century gentleman, but had to be concealed behind a polite facade. There was a game to be played, and the duel was the penalty for being caught failing to play correctly.

This created a situation where a man might have to fight a duel even if he and his opponent very much wanted not to. There was a hierarchy in many areas, whereby some insults could be forgiven after a formal verbal apology, some after a written apology, and some were always grounds for a duel. The injured party could also refuse the apology and choose to fight. As pistols became more popular for duelling, the choice of weapons was given to the challenged party, though many at first thought it reprehensible to fight with handguns.

There were some that thought a pistol duel was safer than a sword fight, since the weapons of the day were very inaccurate and might not fire at all. Once both men had fired the requisite number of shots at one another, honour was considered satisfied unless one or both chose to shoot again. Thus there was a good chance of getting through a pistol duel without being hurt or injuring the opponent, yet with honour intact.

On the other hand, someone was bound to be injured in a sword duel. Some fencing styles approached this realistically, and were not so much about winning a sword fight as about surviving the situation in which the swordsman had to fight a duel. That meant either winning without seriously injuring the opponent or losing in a similarly non-life-threatening manner.

Some fencing masters advocated a very defensive stance, forcing the opponent to commit himself to an attack and then striking him in a manner that would not kill, such as with a thrust to the lead leg or the sword arm. An alternative was to parry and close in, striking with the pommel of the sword. If the opponent was disabled, that was a good outcome. If not, he would probably take the opportunity to deliver some pommel blows of his own.

The swordsman would be hurt, but not too seriously. The opponent, after all, would know that he had been handed a victory that was not bought at the price of a murder trial. Both would live, honour satisfied, and the loser's courage would be commended even if his judgement seemed a bit wayward. This was a strategy of survival geared towards the situation as a whole rather than focusing purely on the combat with swords.

A duel was generally conducted with great politeness and formality. The principals were often forbidden to speak to one another until the duel was resolved. The challenger would appoint his 'friends' to call upon the opponent and deliver the challenge, or perhaps it would be delivered to the friends of the challenged party. A time and place would be agreed, sometimes in great secrecy and sometimes as an open secret. There was a general understanding that nobody would tell the authorities anything and that officials who found out about the matter would pretend they knew nothing unless there was some pressing reason to do otherwise.

On the day of the duel both principals would arrive with their friends, two of whom served as seconds. Their role was to communicate with the seconds of the other party, and thence to the opposing principal. This ritual meant that both men might be speaking within earshot of one another yet passing the message around through a chain of seconds and formally unable to hear what the other said until it were properly relayed.

The seconds were also there to see fair play. In earlier times, it was common for the seconds to join in a duel, creating a six-man brawl that made a wonderful spectacle. By the eighteenth century this was forbidden, though the seconds could act to protect themselves or their principal if necessary. That might occur in the case of an opposing second acting treacherously, or an attempt to strike the principal when he was downed or disarmed.

The duel was started and controlled by a neutral observer appointed as president of the duel. Attacking before the president told the duellists to begin was of course base treachery, as was continuing after the command to halt. Usually a doctor would be present, and quite probably a large crowd of onlookers. This might include officials who would later investigate the affair and report that they could find no evidence that anything had happened. So long as neither participant died, this sort of polite fiction was usually taken at face value. A well-connected individual might force an enquiry to be undertaken, but this was uncommon.

One important factor in the duel was that challenges had to be between peers. Officers of differing military rank could not fight one another, nor could those who were of different social class. The duel could not be used to create a path for advancement or to right an injustice (real or perceived) perpetrated by a superior – that was not desirable to those who held the power in society. What the duel could and did do was to ensure that 'the game' was played the way the key players liked it. It helped maintain a social order within the upper echelons of society, and not coincidentally provided an interesting diversion for those who felt inclined to watch.

Formal rules for the duel were set out at various times, creating versions of the *code duello*. The earliest known example dates from Italy in 1410, and other codes were published later. The Irish *code duello*, published in 1777, was widely adopted in Europe and North America. It was considered a hallmark of a gentleman to have a copy of it in one's pistol case; someone who did not possess the code would not be well regarded, as he might not know how to conduct himself in a matter of honour. The Irish code refers mainly to pistol duelling but its rules are mostly applicable to an encounter with swords.

The Irish code specifies how many times the principals must fire at one another (with pistols) for any given degree of offence – if a blow was struck then at least three shots must be fired at one another before honour is satisfied and an apology can be accepted. With swords, provisions existed for the duel to go on to first blood or until one participant was disarmed or disabled. A principal was generally allowed to 'beg pardon' for his offence after being wounded, but this might not always be granted.

If one principal succeeded in disarming his opponent, he was considered to have won the duel. He might, under some circumstances, require his opponent to take back his weapon and fight on, but this was unusual. He also had the right to break the other man's sword but this was considered to be rather bad form if it were the challenger who was disarmed.

On the other hand, if the challenged party was disarmed he was expected to beg pardon for the offence that gave rise to the duel. If he refused, the challenger was not permitted to kill or wound him, but was entitled to break his sword in this case and could revive the challenge at any time of his choosing.

Duelling Weapons

The small-sword was the standard duelling sword in much of Europe for a great many years, though the pistol gradually supplanted it. However, duelling conventions did vary. There is a tale of a Prussian officer in Paris during 1814, just after the French had been defeated and Napoleon exiled to Elba. This officer wanted to make a name for himself so picked a fight with a French officer.

A duel was arranged, and the Prussian turned up with his curved cutting sword, which was the standard duelling weapon in his home region. The Frenchman arrived with a straight thrusting sword, at which juncture the Prussian objected that the *coup de pointe* was not permitted in duelling.

The response was that thrusting was very much permitted in French duels, and in Paris, even under occupation, the French custom prevailed. The Frenchman would use his thrusting sword and the Prussian could bring whatever he liked to the fight. The Prussian apologised and withdrew his challenge.

Whether or not this event actually occurred, it is an interesting contrast. The Prussian was willing to take the risk of being slashed with a light cutting sword, which would be horribly painful but not likely to be life-threatening, but the prospect of being run through was something else entirely. He was willing to risk serious injury for the sake of a reputation enhanced by a duel, but balked at the idea of being killed over a triviality.

The fleuret (foil) was developed as a training weapon for the small-sword. The term 'foil' essentially meant 'to make safe', for example by rebating the point and blunting the edge of a weapon. A 'foil' could therefore be a foiled rapier used for training, but gradually the term came to refer to a fairly specific implement.

A foil, in this context, was a lighter version of the small-sword. It did not have the highly flexible blade of the modern sporting foil but was broadly similar in terms of length and guard size. The idea behind using a lighter weapon for training was that repeated actions would not be fatiguing, enabling precise training to be undertaken for longer. Fencing with the foil gradually became an art in its own right, and duelling foils were used in some regions.

Although the French school of fencing largely dominated, there was also a strong school of thrust fencing in parts of what is now Germany. The weapon of choice for this system was essentially a sharp version of the training foil suitable for duelling with. University life in eighteenth- and nineteenth-century Germany apparently involved a great deal of duelling, with students fighting over various disputes or for the honour of it.

An insult was required as grounds for the duel, but even here a formality developed. Certain phrases that were not really very insulting could be used when a challenge was desired. This was sufficient to satisfy the requirement for an insult without causing any real offence; presumably the intent was to avoid falling out with the person one wanted to fight with!

Thrust fencing duels were very dangerous, as to win a swordsman had to deliver a potentially fatal thrust. As an alternative, a light cutting weapon could be used. This method has become far more famous in the context of German academic fencing, and developed into a highly stylised combat that was more about character than fencing ability.

Both kinds of duel became known as mensur, though the term is more generally associated with the cutting than the thrusting style. The term originally referred to the measure at which the duel took place; usually there was a quite small area, and the fencers had to remain within it or be considered to have lost through cowardice.

The cutting-sword mensur was responsible for the famous 'duelling scar' associated with upper-class university-educated German men. Wearing heavy protection for the neck, body and eyes, both fencers would fight at close range, with the aim being to deliver a cut to the opponent's face. However, since the acquisition of this scar was the intent, there were benefits to losing so long as the fencer bore the pain of his injury and subsequent treatment without flinching. Medical attention was deliberately rough and ready in order to facilitate the scarring process.

The weapon of choice for this duel was the Schlager, either with a basket hilt (Korbschlager) or a bell-guard (Glockenschlager). Neither had a point, and with the neck and body well protected there was little chance of a fatal injury. However, standing toe to toe with someone trying to slash you around the face was a serious test of character. Disgrace befell those who retreated, flinched or cried out.

The fencing style of the mensur was highly specific, with no movement other than that by the sword arm. A hanging guard position was used, with the well-protected sword arm providing defence from some angles. One requirement of the mensur was that the blades must not stop moving while the bout was in progress.

In addition to various cuts around the head and face, it was also possible to dig the flat end of the sword (the point was cut off square, like a screwdriver) down into the opponent's head from a high hand position and twist it, gouging a lump out of his scalp. Depending on the rules, the combatants either took turns to attack and defend, or simply stood alarmingly close to one another and exchanged blows until either someone was too badly hurt to continue or the requisite number of cuts had been made.

The mensur was often fought in 'rounds' of five cuts by each combatant, with the number of rounds varying. Bouts 160 rounds long have been recorded. Alternatively, a time limit of twenty-five minutes could be imposed. Given the intensity of the action and the close measure, a twenty-five-minute exchange of cuts to the head must have indeed been a great test of character.

The mensur was not confined to Germany, though it was far less common elsewhere. It represented a development of the duel from a means of settling disputes to a way of getting into a rather exclusive club – mensur societies were an ideal place to meet well-connected individuals and secure one's own advantage. The famous scar was, at some times, a requirement for high civil or military rank.

This was, however, a rather unusual situation. In most regions the duel was normally fought with thrusting swords, either small-swords or their descendants. As already noted, the foil was invented as a training tool for the small-sword but was soon used by some duellists. The épée de combat, nowadays usually known as simply the épée, was created later as a counter to the move towards lighter swords.

Épéeists claimed that their weapon more closely paralleled the small-sword, while foilists preferred the quickness of their blades. Duels were fought with both, as well as the traditional duelling sword.

The curious custom of duelling continued for many years, despite attempts to curb it, but gradually the death toll subsided as the duel fell out of fashion. This was more due to social change than any legal intervention; the decline of duelling can be linked to the demise of the social conditions that forced people into fighting over what were often trivial matters.

Leaving aside the modern mensur, which still goes on but is not quite the same thing as a typical duel, duelling faded away during the 1800s but did not entirely disappear for some time after that. Footage exists of the last known sword duel in Europe, which, perhaps fittingly, took place in France. This affair was fought with duelling épées and resulted in only two small wounds, though the experience was undoubtedly extremely intense for both men involved.

Since this time, swordsmanship has been a purely recreational and sporting activity, though the ability to fence is still well regarded in many circles. Fencing is often considered a fairly upmarket or highbrow interest compared with the more usual sports played by greater numbers of people. This impression is today not really accurate; it is a product of the history of fencing rather than its current reality.

CHAPTER 7

Ye True Fyght: Cutting Swords

In 1599, George Silver published his work, *Paradoxes of Defence*, which he proclaimed would prove all of the weaknesses of the rapier and similar weapons and demonstrate how the 'true grounds of fight' were the shorter cutting swords such as the backsword. He also indulged in not a few rants about the evils of false teachers (typically this meant anyone teaching rapier fencing) and foreigners in general.

While Silver had some good points to make about the strengths and weaknesses of the rapier, his observations were hardly objective. He was a raging xenophobe, and the rapier was of course of foreign origin, which hardly created a basis for objective criticism. There was also the fact that most of the rapier play Silver witnessed would not have been of a high standard. The rapier had recently become fashionable in England, and was often carried by gentlemen who had little idea what to do with it.

The available teachers of rapier play, while styling themselves as masters of fence, might well not be very good either in general or with the rapier in particular. There was money to be made from teaching the new weapon, so some instructors of other sword styles jumped on the bandwagon and taught whatever they thought might work. There were some good rapier instructors in England of course, but there were far more who did not really understand how best to use this weapon, and were thus teaching suboptimal technique to students who in any case might not really be interested in becoming excellent swordsmen.

Some of Silver's criticisms were valid. The rapier was large and heavy, and thus not well suited to a fast parry-riposte in the same manner as a small-sword. It was indeed somewhat clumsy on the defence unless used correctly. Once an attack was committed to, the rapier could not quickly change direction if the action turned out to be misjudged. Its length could be a mixed blessing at times; it did give good reach for an attack, but might be a disadvantage at close quarters such as in an alleyway scuffle or on the battlefield.

That all being said, a well-handled rapier was extremely effective, especially under the right circumstances. It was not a battlefield weapon, although it might see use as a sidearm if things went badly wrong, so citing its limitations in that role did not really invalidate it as a tool of personal defence. However, for a close-quarters fight on the battlefield or during a naval boarding action, cutting swords were generally considered to be a better option.

Although a cutting sword is less lethal and has less reach than a thrusting weapon, its threat space is much larger. Rather than being a narrow line in front of the swordsman, a cutting sword's threat space is a bubble around him. Likewise, its wounding envelope is also larger. That is to say, a thrusting sword has to hit with a small point, while travelling in a direction that will cause the point to penetrate at least a couple of inches into the target. A marginal hit will simply scrape flesh and will not produce fight-winning effects.

A cutting sword, on the other hand, can wound even on marginal contact. Its best result will disable or kill an opponent as quickly as a thrust, but it is arguably harder to achieve a killing strike with a cutting weapon than a thrusting one. However, it is much more likely that the swordsman will obtain some useful result from any blow. In a well-controlled duelling situation this might give the advantage to the thrusting sword, but in a chaotic melee the ability to cause some kind of injury even on slight contact may make the cutting weapon more attractive.

A heavy cutting sword can shear limbs clean off or even decapitate the opponent, but even a large and deep cut will not always prove fatal. Similarly, a thrust might be lethal but not immediately so, which could result in the swordsman finding his weapon trapped in the body of a dying but still capable opponent. A cut is less committed in this manner – it can be drawn after impact to both slice and return it to a defensive position, while the thrust has to be pulled straight back out of the target.

The cutting sword thus trades the precise lethality of the sniper rifle for the close-combat effectiveness of the shotgun. Experience over hundreds of years has shown that cutting weapons are generally (but by no means always) preferred for warfare, unless there are considerations such as the need to penetrate heavy armour.

The term given to many cutting swords is 'broadswords', though this is a relatively modern label and was not in use in 1599. A broadsword would qualify as such by virtue of having a broader (and thus heavier) blade than a rapier or similar weapon. A heavy blade translated to greater cutting power, though there were limitations about to how heavy a sword could be and remain useful. For this reason, most broadswords were relatively short, concentrating their weight close to the user's hand.

The Falchion and the Messer

The falchion began to appear some time after AD 1000, and remained in use until the 1500s. It was a simple but highly lethal weapon somewhat resembling a machete with a cross guard. Its heavy, wide blade was designed to deliver powerful hacking strokes in the manner of a meat cleaver or machete. It was single-edged; this was not a weapon well suited to sneaky false-edge cuts.

Blade designs varied, but were typically about 60–65 cm long. Some widened towards the tip; some had a short curved false edge for the last few inches of blade. The purpose in all cases was the same; this was an inexpensive and robust weapon that could be used as a tool when it was not needed for war.

The falchion was a common weapon in the Middle Ages, and is depicted in many scenes from that era. However, few examples survive today. This may be in part because the falchion was a useful tool and would see hard use chopping wood or whatever else needed cutting. It was generally owned by commoners, who would keep using their falchion until it was no longer functional, rather than buying another weapon.

The falchion was primarily carried as a sidearm by infantrymen or archers. Its powerful cutting action was instinctive and needed little training to achieve a reasonable degree of battlefield capability. Obviously, a well-trained swordsman could achieve more with his falchion than someone who just picked it up and started swinging, but since the owners were accustomed to its weight from peacetime use as a tool, the falchion put a potent weapon in many hands, and did so cheaply.

It is thought that many knights favoured the falchion, even though it was generally considered a commoner's weapon. This is possibly because the falchion's blade was sufficiently heavy to shear through limbs or pike hafts and to penetrate most armour. However, it may be that depictions of falchions in use by armoured warriors have been misinterpreted. Not all armoured warriors were knights; some would be professional soldiers of the middle classes. It is possible that at least some depictions of a knight with his falchion were in fact one of these social inferiors.

Social considerations aside, the falchion was a good choice for the battlefield. Short enough to be handy in a close-quarters melee, it could still deliver a heavy enough blow to disable even an armoured opponent. It might be used with a shield by some troops, but archers and the like would find themselves fighting with little or no armour and no shield, and armed with a sword that was not well suited to defence.

Aggressive tactics and opportunism were the only answer; the falchion-armed footsoldier would strike at whatever targets presented themselves, and would hope to eliminate his opponents before they could launch an effective attack of their own. In a close melee, this would often mean striking at opponents from behind or from the flank, which would be facilitated by the poor field of view afforded by a heavy helm.

At such close quarters, a knight might not be able to see an opponent who was well positioned to strike, making his own defence a problem. His answer, too, was to press forward aggressively and to attack what was in front of him, hoping not to be struck down from the flank. Thus, surviving a medieval melee could well be less about swordsmanship and more a question of luck. If so, the odds were stacked in favour of members of the most numerous, aggressive and well-armoured side as well as those who possessed the most effective weapons for such a scramble.

This is the nature of large-scale close combat; there are many variables beyond the swordsman's control. He cannot know what is going on behind him, and even the best could be struck by an unseen opponent. The threat space of a rapidly moving cutting sword might assist his chances of survival by deterring opponents who might otherwise rush in from the flank, whereas a thrusting weapon was less threatening, except directly to the swordsman's front.

A similar weapon to the falchion appeared in Germany from the fourteenth century onward. Known as a messer ('knife'), or langes messer ('long knife'), it was essentially a single-edged sword-like weapon whose blade was shaped like that of a knife. The hilt, too, was much like that of a knife, with the exception of a small amount of hand protection, meaning that the messer could be owned by commoners, despite a legal restriction on swords in common hands.

The messer's hand protection was of unusual design. In addition to projections creating a small crosspiece guard, the messer also had a third projection called the nagel (nail) at right angles to the blade. The nagel was used to catch an opponent's blade in the manner of quillions on a standard crosspiece guard.

Variations on the messer concept existed, ranging from overgrown knives to two-handed weapons, and from knife-like blades to curved weapons resembling a sabre. Although, like the falchion, the messer was associated with commoners, it was not uncommon to find examples in the possession of noblemen.

Manuals covering the use of the messer include the Glasgow *Fechtbuch*, which dates from 1508 and deals with longsword fighting, grappling and dagger use as well as the messer. The material in such manuals acknowledges that the most likely encounter with one will be in the hands of a commoner who may not have had any training. His attacks would be simple, though obviously deadly if they landed.

Thus, instruction with the messer began with how to deal with a 'peasant's strike', straight down from the shoulder, and proceeded through a series of increasingly complex and advanced techniques presented as plays. A play was a logical sequence of movements, with the opponent's most likely reaction setting up the next move. Plays could be practised as a set piece, or broken down into their constituent parts.

Messer play, like many weapons, included a significant amount of grappling and wrestling. The opponent could be taken to the ground and thus made vulnerable to a finishing move with the messer, or thrown to the ground to injure him. It is possible to overestimate the importance of grappling in messer and other combat systems, however. Some manuals devote a great deal of space to descriptions and plates illustrating grappling moves, and relatively little to actions with the blade.

This does not mean that grappling was the main part of the system, merely that explaining its complexities required a lot of space. Blade use, in most cases, was fairly simple in terms of technique, with advanced applications being mainly a matter of training. A set of blade actions that could be presented in a few pages might lead to endless applications and combinations, but these would be made up of the same basic components.

It was not all that desirable for a master to record too many of his plays and advanced concepts; others would study them and develop counters, or steal them and teach them as their own. Better to present the core strokes and positions of the system in a treatise, and teach the applications to those willing to pay for instruction.

Messer combat could be very basic – swinging a heavy blade is fairly instinctive, and close-quarters stabbing was always an option – or could be extremely sophisticated. A skilled swordsman learned to make use of the Nagel to perform unique defences and to trap an opponent's blade, and his weapon offered him a wide range of options. Long enough to give a reasonable amount of reach yet handy at close quarters, the Messer could shear through protection and deliver terrible wounds, creating an excellent weapon that was a sword in all but name.

The Cutlass and the Hanger

For the commoner, weapons that could also be used as tools (or vice versa) offered significant advantages. Blades, even of mediocre quality, were not cheap. Thus to those whose primary business was not warfare, a weapon that could earn its keep on the farm or in the hunt was more desirable than a specialist sword.

This also applied at sea, and accounts for the popularity of the cutlass as a naval sidearm. The cutlass was a single-edged weapon, the blade often but not always curved, with a very basic hand guard. Its heavy blade was well suited to chopping through a variety of materials as well as flesh. Cutlasses could be used as tools for work or emergency damage control, cutting away ropes or debris that impeded the crew or threatened the ship. They could also be used to cut the ropes attached to enemy boarding grapples.

The cutlass was sometimes referred to as a 'butcher's blade', and certainly it was an uncomplicated weapon. Naval crews were drilled in use of the cutlass en masse rather than as individual swordsmen – nobody expected a common sailor to learn to fence, even if he somehow found the time. Instead a group of men armed with cutlasses would advance aggressively, chopping at whomever presented himself in front of them. A combination of vigour and aggression would, hopefully, ensure that casualties fell more on the enemy than the cutlass party, and thus a boarding action could be won by a sort of rigged numbers game.

At its simplest, cutlass drill might be nothing more than a mechanical set of movements revolving around a steady advance with a cut on each step. Down, then backhand across, then down again. Defence was not generally a factor in such drills; individual welfare was subordinated to the concept of pitting one crew against another. Often, the most important factors were not so much the quality of cutlass play but agility and skill at moving about aboard ship.

Marines and some members of a crew might be expected to train more extensively, though the musket and bayonet were the primary weapons of the former. Later generations swapped their muskets for rifles and might be issued revolvers, but the cutlass remained a useful weapon aboard ship for a number of reasons. It was handy at close quarters and much better suited to a boarding action than a naval officer's dress small-sword. It was also less likely to catch on rigging or timbers in the close confines of a ship.

The cutlass was also a very intimidating weapon. A small-sword might mark the wearer as a gentleman of some importance and perhaps a skilled swordsman, but a cutlass spoke of intent to kill. Sentries or shore patrols equipped with cutlasses provided an effective deterrent to troublemakers.

The cutlass remains a ceremonial weapon for naval personnel, but fell out of use early in the twentieth century. The United States Navy received its last model of cutlass in 1917, but few ever saw use other than on guard duty and ceremonial occasions. A handful of Royal Navy cutlasses were broken out of storage in 1940 and issued to Home Guard personnel for lack of anything better. This is more indicative of how bad things were early in the Second World War than of any confidence in the effectiveness of these weapons.

Up until the late nineteenth century, what today would be termed a cutlass might equally be referred to as a hanger. The terms were more or less interchangeable, though today 'cutlass' has naval connotations and 'hanger' typically means a landsman's weapon. Both had a similar form and function; hangers were carried as tools when working or hunting. Someone in the habit of carrying a hanger when about his business would never lack a useable weapon, but would not attract the same notice as he might when going armed with a combat sword.

A hanger, sometimes referred to as a sabre-briquet, was issued to some infantry as a sidearm during the eighteenth and nineteenth centuries. This was not a particularly successful move, partly because the infantryman's primary weapon, his musket (with bayonet fixed), was sufficiently effective in hand-to-hand combat that a sidearm was not really needed.

There was also the factor that many military hangers were of poor design or manufacture and little use in a fight.

French troops of the Napoleonic era generally considered that their hangers were useful only for chopping wood for the fire. This sentiment was shared by those of later periods and other nations. The French artillery issued a short-sword in 1831 that somewhat resembled a Roman gladius. The fact that it was known as a 'cabbage chopper' by its users says a lot about how well it was regarded. A similar weapon issued to American artillery crews in the Civil War era was equally despised.

Although hangers were not generally well regarded as weapons, they were useful as tools. Wood (and perhaps cabbages) might need chopping every day in the field, so possession of a suitable tool was an asset. For personnel whose main task was work rather than combat, the hanger was often indispensable. Many units of sappers and pioneers were equipped with hangers, often with a saw-toothed top edge. These were tools that might be pressed into use as weapons rather than the other way around, and were a useful part of the pioneer's field equipment.

The Backsword and the Broadsword

The backsword, a single-edged broadsword-type weapon, was one of the most effective and successful swords ever developed. Characterised by a basket hilt offering excellent hand protection and a blade designed for heavy, shearing cuts, the backsword was easier to produce than a double-edged weapon, and very strong, as the spine of the blade (the side opposite the cutting edge) could be much thicker than an edge that needed to be sharpened.

Backswords typically had a short false edge for opportunistic cuts, and an entirely useful point, but their purpose was to deliver powerful blows that originated from the shoulder. Blade lengths varied considerably, with 75–85 cm being fairly common. Longer blades were used; the British Federation for Historical Swordplay allows blades of up to 37 inches in its tournaments to reflect this.

The backsword could be used for personal defence, but it was a highly effective battlefield weapon either on its own or when paired with a targe (small shield) or a dirk. Backswords were used by both infantry and cavalry of various nations, with variants on the concept existing in many nations.

The Scottish Highland broadsword began to appear in the early 1700s. It was a very similar weapon to the backsword, although only some were true backswords (i.e. they had a single edge and a thick spine backing the blade); others were double-edged broadswords that could 'cut both ways'. This term, which became a figure of speech, probably referred to the fact that a broadswordsman could cut down and then pull his spent cut back up along the same path without turning his sword, enabling him to make a very fast follow-up cut after a failed attack.

The key to using a heavy-bladed sword, especially when it was used for both attack and defence, was to make use of its mass rather than fighting against it. Thus, high, hanging guards were favoured by many backsword instructors. Although tiring for those not conditioned to the weapon, a hanging guard positioned the sword to attack or defend as necessary, utilising gravity as it descended, rather than fighting it to get into position when time was short. With a cut coming in or when presented with a fleeting opportunity, the advantage of position was an important one.

Other backsword guards were fairly conventional, though the resting guard was anything but. The sword arm was passed across in front of the body with the blade pointing behind. The elbow of the sword arm was supported by holding it with the off hand. This position gave the swordsman the look of someone clutching at a belly wound or perhaps nursing a severe case of indigestion, but had the advantage of allowing the sword arm to rest while keeping the weapon ready for action.

A sword held in the resting guard could be brought rapidly back to a hanging guard by simply letting go of the elbow with the off hand and pulling it upwards as if drawing the sword from its scabbard. The same action could be performed as an upward cut under the sword arm or a defensive action to stop a descending cut made by the opponent. Despite its name the resting guard was not a 'guard position' in the sense that it closed off some lines of attack, but can be considered more of a ready position that gave distinct advantages when used properly.

The resting guard was not a position that would be used when an opponent was in close proximity, unless the swordsman was trying to tempt his opponent into committing himself to an attack. It was an expedient that allowed a swordsman to take a rest when possible and also perhaps a psychological gambit. Taking the sword behind him was a gesture of great confidence on the part of the swordsman and might intimidate an opponent.

The use of a heavy-bladed sword affected the timings of attack and defence. A well-handled backsword could change direction alarmingly fast and attack with great speed, but its momentum meant that once committed, a cut or parry would require a significant amount of time to accomplish. A skilled swordsman could exploit this by feinting or otherwise encouraging his opponent to commit to an action, then deceiving it to hit elsewhere.

With heavy-bladed weapons there is often enough delay for the swordsman to realise that he has been 'had' and that there is no possible way to get to the real cut in time to stop it. The author can attest that even with practice weapons this is a most uncomfortable moment; the sheer horror of it in a bout with live blades can only be imagined.

The use of body movement to change the dynamics of a cut or parry was very important when fighting with a backsword or similar weapon. A small movement could be enough to make the difference between a parry succeeding or not getting there in time. Moving away from the attack (to the side or by retreating) either increased the time available for a defence or reduced the distance the sword must move in order to make a parry – effectively making the parry quicker. The effect was the same in both cases; use of movement affected timing.

The weight of the weapons involved also affected timing in a fight. A backswordsman might well find himself engaged with another backsword or a similar weapon, whose timing would be well matched to his own. Depending on the place and time, however, he might find himself up against a rapier or small-sword, or some other weapon entirely. This changed the nature of the fight considerably.

A thrusting sword typically had longer reach than a backsword, especially in the case of the rapier, so the backswordsman would generally try to sweep or bash it aside before closing in. Once inside the reach of the rapier, i.e. 'past the point', the backswordsman was in a far better position than the rapier-armed fencer. This was in part what Silver alluded to in *Paradoxes of Defence*; the rapier was a big target to be struck aside with a beat or its heavier equivalent, the 'batter' favoured by some styles.

However, a skilled rapier fencer was entirely aware that his opponent would want to do this, and was adept at avoiding attempts to bash his blade around. He might well take advantage of the backsword's heavily committed blow to avoid it, and thrust before the backswordsman could regain control of his weapon and defend himself. The rapier fencer had his own system of body mechanics to get his point back on line – and he had two good cutting edges of his own.

Where the backswordsman's problem in defeating a rapier was in covering the distance required to strike his opponent, if he came up against a small-sword he had a different set of circumstances to deal with. The small-sword moved very fast and could easily slip around attempts to find and engage it or beat it aside. A well-timed thrust could arrive before the backswordsman had time to respond, and even a badly timed one might result in mutual injury.

The Scottish soldier Donald MacBane considered this problem in his 1728 manual *The Expert Swordsman's Companion*. MacBane was a rather quarrelsome fellow who seemed to be able to get into a fight almost anywhere. His military career as a professional soldier took him all over the Continent, in service with various masters, and when not fighting wars he duelled over various large and small matters.

MacBane would fight with anyone over anything, it seemed. During his service with the Earl of Angus' regiment, an incident occurred that reflects the culture of the times: MacBane mortally wounded his immediate superior (a corporal) in a duel, and had to flee to avoid the death penalty for murder. He was, however, assisted by his dying victim, who gave him money to facilitate his escape, and by the captain of his company. The affair of honour outweighed the rule of law in many eyes, which was as well for MacBane and others like him. His last duel was fought in 1726 with a falchion rather than the more usual small-sword or backsword. Two years later he published his thoughts on swordsmanship.

All this experience gave MacBane a solid insight into how best to go about fighting with the small-sword, the broadsword and other weapons besides, and against various opponents. Some of his advice is perhaps questionable, such as the idea that a folded damp handkerchief placed under the hat will ward off blows from a broadsword, but overall MacBane understood the swordsmanship of the duel and the battlefield.

MacBane, along with William Hope, was one of the first to refer to the 'broad sword' as such. He discusses a situation where he had a small-sword and his opponent 'a broad'. The term 'sheering-sword' is also used in manuals from this era, presumably to refer to the heavy cutting weapons.

One basic rule of the small-sword *v.* backsword encounter is that the swordsman with the heavier weapon wants blade contact; the man armed with the lighter sword would prefer to avoid it. If the small-swordsman can force the backswordsman to move his weapon around looking for the blade, these movements will inevitably become ever larger due to the weight of the weapon, creating an opportunity to launch an attack. On the other hand, the heavier weapon will knock a small-sword aside with ease.

A simple gambit for the backswordsman was to try to hit the small-sword near the middle of the blade and smash it. A small-sword could successfully parry a much heavier blade providing the principle of defence was followed, i.e. the attack was met with the forte of the blade as close to the hilt as possible. However, a blow that found the middle part of the blade would at least knock the small-sword far to the side and might well snap it.

The ability to apply psychology and 'read' the opponent was also useful. If the backswordsman were confident that his opponent would react defensively, he could storm forward aggressively, making heavy cuts and generally trying to intimidate his opponent. Once the small-swordsman was forced to defend, his weapon could likely be battered down or knocked aside. The danger here was that the opponent would not oblige by trying to make a series of desperate parries. If he was able to evade and counter-attack, or even if he simply panicked and stuck his arm out, there was a danger that the overly aggressive backswordsman would run on to a point.

Since a victory won at the price of death or serious injury was not worth much, the backswordsman would typically be fairly cautious unless he was sure he could intimidate his opponent into behaving predictably. A fight between mismatched weapons of this sort would often be quite short, or at least would have little in the way of interplay between the blades. There might be a quite lengthy period of searching for an advantage, but once one combatant or the other committed to an attack it would usually be over fast. The trick, as always, was knowing when to commit and when to pass up what might well look like a good opportunity to a less skilled swordsman.

A metal practice sword would have to be of fairly high quality to withstand the endless parries and cuts of backsword play, and thus would cost as much as a fighting weapon. A cheap alternative was the singlestick, a stick of roughly the same length as a backsword and fitted with a wickerwork hand guard. Singlesticking was not only practice for sword combat, but became a sport in its own right.

The rules of singlestick combat have varied over time. It became a popular spectacle at English county fairs, along with wrestling. By the late 1700s, the aim in a competitive bout was to 'break the head' of an opponent, i.e. to draw blood from the head. Blows landing elsewhere did not score, but could be used to weaken the opponent and wear him down. Parries and ripostes were used in the manner of backsword play; a skilled singlestick player could easily defend himself from an enthusiastic but inept opponent, striking wherever he would until he felt it was time to win.

This sort of entertainment kept a significant number of fighting-men employed. Prize bouts would be arranged, much as with boxing or wrestling, either as the main event or as part of a programme of violent entertainment. The most famous of these entertainers was James Figg, who was born in 1684 or 1695; sources vary on the exact date. Figg fought for money with the staff, singlestick and backsword as well as in brutal bare-knuckle fights, and became a legend in the field.

Having carved out a name for himself, Figg attracted large numbers of students to learn from him. He taught what he called the 'noble science of defence', often to gentlemen and aristocrats, and gave exhibitions of his skill at arms. Others did much the same thing, but never achieved the same level of fame as Figg.

Singlesticking remained popular as a sport and as training for the backsword or the naval cutlass until the middle of the 1800s, after which it declined. The art was kept alive by a few specialist groups, notably military academies and fencing instructors with an interest in the history of the art, and today is seeing something of a revival as interest in western martial arts increases.

Broadswords on Horseback

The backsword and a variety of broadswords were also used from horseback. Their heavy blades, driven by gravity and the movement of a horse, would deliver extremely potent cuts against infantry and cavalry alike. Numerous designs of cavalry broadsword existed, among them the pallasch. This was a weapon generally associated with eastern Europe, though it was also adopted for the British heavy cavalry.

A pallasch was essentially a long, single-edged cutting sword that might have a basket hilt or a simpler hand guard. Sometimes referred to as a 'heavy cavalry broadsword', this weapon was designed to be used very aggressively. Cavalrymen did sometimes become engaged in melees with other cavalry, which would necessitate a certain amount of what might be termed 'horseback fencing', but more commonly they struck as they passed the target.

Against infantry this was generally a matter of striking down at heads and shoulders. The shako worn by many nations' infantry in the Napoleonic era was allegedly developed to create headgear capable of providing good defence against a downward sword blow. Infantry who fled could be hacked from behind by horsemen, who would find it easy to catch up, but infantry who stood their ground with mounted bayonets, whether singly or in a well-organised formation, were a much tougher prospect.

The art of fighting from horseback against a bayonet-armed infantryman (and vice versa) was difficult to teach, but drills were developed, and at times fencing matches were arranged that pitted a musketeer (or later a rifleman) against a cavalryman. Sabre *v.* bayonet fencing became a competitive sport in the British Army, albeit not a very widespread one. In general, however, this situation was best avoided by sword-armed cavalrymen. It was not a good place for either infantry or cavalry to be, and in all likelihood the advantage lay with the infantryman who kept his cool and used his bayonet well. If he had the cover of an obstacle or was part of a large formation presenting a hedge of bayonets, then in practice there was little the mounted swordsman could do.

An encounter with another horseman would generally be fleeting; two horsemen charging at one another might well engage in what amounted to a game of chicken, each trying to convince the other that he was going to cut or thrust no matter what. If one cut and the other defended, they would be past one another before a riposte could be made. Both deciding to defend would also result in a bloodless passing.

If both decided to attack, chances were good that both would be seriously injured. There is an account of an English cavalryman standing up in his stirrups and cutting down so hard that he clove his French opponent's brass helmet and skull open down to the collarbone, but unfortunately this occurred just after he had impaled himself on the Frenchman's thrusting sabre point. Both, naturally, died immediately.

In general, an encounter between two cavalry forces meeting head-on resulted in very few casualties at first contact. Each man chose whether to attack or defend, and the difficulty of delivering an attack against a ready opponent was such that most blows would be parried or would otherwise not land. It was not uncommon in the Napoleonic era for two cavalry squadrons to pass through one another and emerge with virtually no casualties.

However, if a melee began then things were rather different. The initial clash might produce few effective blows, but as horsemen encountered subsequent ranks of the opposing regiment or wheeled about to strike at new targets, then a situation prevailed not very different to the medieval melee discussed earlier in this chapter.

Many blows struck in a cavalry melee would be opportunistically delivered from the flank or rear. As armour became less common, cavalrymen were increasingly vulnerable to this kind of attack, which was one reason for the reintroduction of armour in some countries during the Napoleonic era. The French chose to give their heavy cavalry back- and breastplates; their Austrian equivalents wore only a breastplate. This was lighter and cheaper to provide, and gave just as much protection during the charge, but created a disadvantage in a melee. Most nations, however, provided no body protection to their cavalry.

Landing a blow in a cavalry melee was a complicated business. The cavalry trooper had to guide and control his mount amid the noise and chaos of combat, getting close enough to deliver a blow and with his mount oriented such that he could strike effectively. Mounted swordsmanship was thus as much about the quality of the horse and its training, and the rider's horsemanship, as it was about control of the sword. There was also the added complication of the horse's head and flanks; a cavalryman had to avoid injuring his own mount or entangling his weapon in his reins.

Small wonder, then, that most nations chose to arm their heavy cavalry with heavy broadswords. Complex fencing exchanges would be very rare if they happened at all; most often it was a matter of timing a single cut or a single parry to occur at a fleeting instant of contact. Naturally a sword was chosen that would maximise the effects of a blow against a fleeing infantryman or a passing cavalry trooper.

The English heavy cavalry adopted the pallasch in 1796. Its designer, John le Marchant, preferred a curved sabre but was overruled by the senior officers of the British cavalry. They had decided that a straight sword was desirable for the heavy cavalry, so a copy of the Austrian pallasch was adopted. It was one of the least subtle swords ever issued, being extremely poorly suited to parrying, feinting or doing much besides acting as a sharp-edged club.

Many of these weapons were later adapted by grinding their 'hatchet point' (this refers to a straight diagonal tip, not any resemblance to an axe blade) into a more effective spear-point shape. Although this measure did enable the pallasch to thrust, it remained a clumsy and unwieldy weapon.

Le Marchant, among many of his contemporaries, considered that the design of a sword was only a minor factor in determining the effectiveness of cavalry on the battlefield. Horsemanship training and the quality of mounts available were far more important. Essentially, factors that put a cavalryman in a position to strike a blow were far more important than the weapon he struck with.

The Sabre

It is quite hard to pin down a definition of exactly what is (and what is not) a sabre. The term is often understood to mean a single-edged, curved sword associated with cavalry, but there were also straight sabres and infantry sabres. Most, but not all, were cutting swords.

The sabre, or a sabre-like weapon, has been identified as far back as the ninth or even the sixth century AD. These weapons were used by mounted warriors originating east of Europe, and followed a variety of broadly similar designs. The scimitar or shamshir of the Middle East and the shaska of the Caucasus are probably descended from the same family of weapons.

These weapons used a curved blade and generally had a minimal or no hand guard. The curve of the blade served two purposes; it concentrated the force of a blow at the weapon's 'point of percussion' for maximum effect, and also ensured that whatever part of the blade struck the target, it would slide and slice into flesh. This was especially useful from horseback, as the smallest contact of blade would create a serious wound due to the movement of the horse.

These weapons gradually evolved into a weapon recognisable as a 'modern' sabre, which was at first popular in Poland, Hungary and other regions of eastern Europe. Typically the blade was single-edged, perhaps with a short false edge, and very much designed to cut rather than thrust. Blades were often sharply curved and quite heavy, creating a weapon that was well suited to hard blows that would penetrate most protection.

The sabre gradually spread across Europe, largely due to the influence of Hungarian hussars. These were irregular light cavalry raised in the late 1400s from local tribes for service with the Austro-Hungarian army.

Hussars were later hired as mercenaries for service throughout Europe, and over time evolved into armoured heavy cavalry armed with lances. In Poland and Lithuania, and some other regions besides, hussar formations remained as heavy cavalry but elsewhere they gradually returned to their original form of irregular light horsemen.

The distinctive flamboyant dress of these troops, and their effectiveness on the battlefield, resulted in widespread emulation. There was a general move towards a curved sword for cavalry, particularly light cavalry, which was driven as much by fashion as effectiveness. Nations that had nothing in common with Hungary or eastern Europe began to raise their own hussar formations, dressing them in an ostentatious manner that contrasted with the somewhat more military dress of other light cavalry.

By the time of the French Revolution and the Napoleonic Wars that followed, various types of cavalry existed in Europe. The main split was between heavy cavalry intended to charge the enemy and break his lines and the light cavalry who could also launch a powerful charge but were in addition used as scouts, foragers and to pursue a defeated opponent. In practice, the situation was more complex than this.

Most nations had heavy cavalry of some kind. These were big men on big horses, and armed with big swords. Some nations, such as France and Austria, provided body armour to the heavy cavalry; others did not, although a helmet was generally issued. Heavy cavalry were sometimes referred to as cuirassiers (for their cuirass, or breastplate) though many nations used the local form of the term 'heavy cavalry'.

British heavy cavalry were, perhaps confusingly, called dragoons. This had its origins in an economy measure; dragoon regiments were paid less than heavy cavalry as they were of lower status, so all heavy cavalry units were redesignated as dragoons to reduce costs. The dragoon regiments continued to carry out the heavy cavalry role, so in Britain the term dragoon came to mean 'heavy cavalry' whereas elsewhere it retained its more traditional meaning.

The word dragoon derives from dragon, the term for a short musket in use in the 1600s. Dragoons were initially infantrymen mounted on cheap, low-quality horses for mobility and used to secure bridges or other necessary points ahead of an advance. In time, dragoons evolved into a sort of medium cavalry who in theory could also fight on foot. In revolutionary and Napoleonic France they gained a helmet and were heavy cavalry in all but name.

Light cavalry included lancers in those nations that used them plus sword-armed light horsemen designated as hussars, chasseurs à cheval or simply light cavalry. The light horseman's weaponry included a carbine and perhaps two or more pistols as well as his sabre. The carbine was an effective weapon, and there was much debate about whether it was best to deal with an enemy cavalry unit by halting to shoot or countercharging with the sword. The pistol, on the other hand, was less useful.

Even the mature flintlock technology of the early 1800s was unreliable at best, and attempting to hit anything from horseback with a pistol – if it discharged at all – was something of a lottery. Many cavalrymen considered that their pistols had the same effective range as their sabres, and since the sabre could be used to strike repeatedly and to parry with, it was very much the preferred weapon.

Although light cavalry were equipped to skirmish with carbines, the ideal was the sabre charge, boot to boot, in successive lines. A cavalry regiment would typically deploy in three lines, with squadrons delivering a charge then breaking off as the next moved up. Repeated shocks could break an enemy unit more effectively than a single attack, and prevented the cavalry from becoming embroiled in a melee.

For this kind of action the cavalryman needed a sword that gave him good reach and struck hard. The French heavy cavalry favoured straight thrusting sabres, which required a specialised technique for use at the charge. The cavalryman had to learn to allow his arm to be pulled behind him as he passed the stricken target, dragging his weapon back out of the victim, after which it was returned to a forward position. He was of course somewhat vulnerable during this period, but he was also moving fast and unlikely to be attacked.

This manner of using the sabre as a lance was popular with the French heavy cavalry, but not with most other nations. It was certainly effective, especially against infantry, but these heavy swords were at a disadvantage in a melee against lighter, handier swords. At the Battle of Austerlitz in 1805 the French heavy cavalry, who liked to sing insulting songs about the hussars, got into trouble during a melee with Austrian cavalry and had to be rescued by the hussars. It is recorded that they did not cease singing their songs afterward, but they had rather less fervour to them.

The English heavy cavalry, as already noted, favoured the straight cutting sword, as did the Austrian formations it was copied from. Lighter cavalry tended to be issued curved swords, whose form was broadly similar across Europe in 1800 or so. The French cavalry moved entirely to curved sabres from 1822 onward, and curved weapons became standard in most armies for the rest of the century.

The typical light cavalry sabre of 1800 was single-edged, with a short false edge and a usable point. It was not too sharply curved to thrust, and had a simple hilt consisting of a stirrup-shaped knuckle bow and a minimal hand guard in the form of a disc or small crosspiece. One of the finest examples of the type was the English 1796 pattern light cavalry sabre designed by John le Marchant. Although he had wanted this weapon to be adopted by all cavalry, the heavy units received the clumsy pallasch instead.

By this time, the technique of the cutting sword had reached a fairly standard form in many areas. This was largely derived from the backsword, though it worked entirely as well with the sabre. There were six main cuts, usually defined by the manner of delivery rather than the target. Thus an English cavalryman who was making a downward forehand cut at an opponent's head was using Cut One. Another man who – for whatever reason – was cutting down in a forehand blow at an opponent's knee was still making Cut One.

The standard British system considered forehand cuts to be odd numbered, backhand cuts to be even. One and two were downward (usually directed at the head, shoulder and neck), three and four were upward (under the sword arm, to the flank or on foot to the hip area), five and six were horizontal. Some systems differentiated between cuts made at face, chest and belly height, others considered all to be cuts five and six. Cut seven, straight down, was rarely used, and cut eight, directly upwards, was impossible on horseback.

Only one thrust was included in the British cavalry manual. Often referred to as the 'downward thrust against infantry', this was made with the true edge of the blade up and the false edge down, and was delivered with a plunging action. It could also be used on foot, along with thrusts in tierce and quarte. Thrusting was very much secondary to cutting, however.

The Sabre on Foot

Although the sabre is generally associated with cavalry, it was adopted by officers of the British light infantry from the late 1790s onwards. This trend occurred because light infantry units often operated quite dispersed.

An officer of a 'line' unit was protected by his company or battalion, and was quite unlikely to have to personally engage the enemy. A light infantry officer, whether engaged in skirmishing, scouting or an assault, might find himself in need of an effective battlefield sword.

Initially these officers simply bought themselves light cavalry sabres, but from 1803 onwards steps were taken to produce a standard light infantry sabre. An infantry sabre was, ideally, a little shorter and lighter than a cavalry sabre. It had to be capable of fencing rather than slashing at an opponent as the user rode past. Whereas a cavalryman had a very short engagement time with most opponents, an infantry officer had to stand and fight. His weapon had to stay under control and be able to exploit any openings that presented themselves.

The system of using these infantry sabres was not very much different to that used with cavalry weapons, although since there was no longer a need to worry about carving pieces off the officer's own horse, he could employ a wider range of strokes. These lighter sabres could also be used with a rolling action, with movements coming from the forearm, rather than swinging it from the shoulder.

The key principle of military sabre combat was that so long as the hand guard remained inside what is sometimes termed 'the box', the user could defend and attack effectively. The box was defined by the user's shoulder and hip joints; so long as the hilt of the weapon stayed in an area just a little wider than this, the blade could be quickly moved to any place it needed to be in order to parry or deliver a cut. This was only the case with relatively light sabres of course; a heavy cavalry weapon was used more in the manner of a backsword.

The military sabre saw action far beyond the European battlefields, and encountered a wide range of opposition, including spears, assegais, various exotic sword weapons, hatchets and clubs. As the nineteenth century went on, cartridge firearms became ever more effective, and the sword declined in usefulness. It remained effective in the 'small wars' of the colonial era for the same reason that light infantry officers adopted the sabre – small forces might be caught far from support, and an officer could not always rely on the protection of a large force of riflemen.

During the colonial era, it was not uncommon for an officer to have his sword in his strong hand and a revolver in the other. One common – if hardly fair – technique was to parry an assailant's attack with the sabre and shoot him with the revolver. However, since there was little chance to reload in a close action, shots had to be husbanded for an emergency.

One interesting piece of advice when confronted by an enemy swordsman was to engage his blade. If his engagement was heavy and clumsy, the advice was to fight him with the sword. If he engaged in a light and subtle manner, the officer should shoot him since he was obviously a skilled swordsman.

The Last Hurrah

The sabre was the last European sword weapon to see extensive use on the battlefield. It became a standard sidearm for officers of infantry and artillery in various nations, although arms in some nations continued to prefer a small-sword. It was not uncommon, for example, for officers of infantry or cavalry to carry a different weapon from that used by artillery officers. This was not always driven by concerns about battlefield effectiveness; fashion played a significant part in choosing the weapons worn in dress uniform and even on the battlefield.

By the mid-nineteenth century, this was not too much of a problem. The sword was becoming increasingly an anachronism, of little use on the battlefield. Duels were typically fought with pistols, making swordsmanship something of an irrelevance even for military officers. Sword drill was important for the parade ground, and so survived long after practical applications were forgotten.

That said, the author has fought with sabres against a British officer who knew nothing more than formal sword drill. Despite having no training in how to fight and (apparently) no concept of defence whatsoever, this individual was nonetheless a dangerous opponent. His powerful cuts and win-or-die attitude made him a formidable aggressor, who could only be overcome by superior skill and a defensive style aimed at waiting for an opening for a riposte or a stop cut.

This is perhaps not historically inaccurate; it is certainly harder to train swordsmen to defend successfully than to attack. The aggressive swordsman only has to get lucky once, whereas the defender has to get it right every time until he can land his own blow. However, this is the only game in town – if both combatants are on the all-out offensive, mutual death is the most likely outcome.

Advancing firearm technology had numerous implications for the swordsman on the battlefield. The percussion cap made weapons more reliable and quicker to fire, but there were still significant limitations. A multi-barrel 'pepperbox' pistol or a revolver offered several shots, but would take too long to reload to be much use once discharged. Besides, it was not unknown for an officer to empty his revolver into an assailant who yet lived long enough to kill him. A sword offered the chance to defend as well as make dramatic gestures that did not have the same impact when made with a handgun.

Thus the sword remained a useful military sidearm during the first half of the nineteenth century. In the hands of the cavalry, it was anything but decisive, however. Despite the weight and power of the cavalry sabre, it was possible to gain significant protection by using a rolled cloak positioned in a horseshoe shape over the left shoulder and across the torso. A heavy greatcoat – especially when wet – was also effective against many cuts.

This reflected in part the poor design of many military swords in the era, and also declining standards of swordsmanship. Several nations adopted weapons only to discard them after a few years as unfit for their purpose, with cavalry troopers sometimes unfortunate enough to have to fight a war with these weapons.

The Battle of Balaclava, fought in 1854 as part of the Crimean War, provides a snapshot of the fate of cavalry at the time. The Light Brigade is famous for its charge against Russian artillery, and actually succeeded in overrunning some batteries before being driven off, but achieved nothing of importance, mainly due to being given an inappropriate mission. As is the way of such things, this gallant failure has become famous, while two notable victories achieved during the same action are all but forgotten.

A charge of Russian cavalry towards Balaclava itself was shot to pieces by the rifles of the 93rd Highlanders – the famous 'thin red streak tipped with steel' – and never came close enough for that steel to see use. Soon afterwards, the Heavy Brigade of British cavalry charged uphill against three times its number of Russian cavalry and drove them off. This latter action involved almost 2,000 horsemen in a lengthy melee, and resulted in around 110 killed and wounded on the British side to about 250 among their Russian opponents.

The vast majority of the casualties – around 90 per cent on the British side and nearer 80 per cent on the Russian – were wounded rather than killed, despite being hacked at by heavy cavalry sabres for an extended period. Some of the British troopers recorded that their swords would turn in their hand upon striking a Russian greatcoat; slippery brass grips were blamed in other campaigns for similar difficulty in delivering a decisive blow.

Limitations of the swords in use aside, Balaclava serves as an example of how cavalry had become increasingly ineffective during the nineteenth century, at least when attempting to charge with the sword. The mathematics of the situation were pitiless; ground could only be crossed so fast, and infantry could shoot faster and more accurately than ever before. Cavalry had to advance in the face of fire that started earlier and caused more casualties than ever before, until it became virtually impossible to come to handstrokes.

Much the same happened to infantry equipped with hand weapons such as spears or swords during the colonial wars. Suicidal bravery could not stop bullets; steady infantry could shoot a charge apart and remain in close formation to repel any stragglers who reached sword range. To some extent, this situation had existed for some time. During the Napoleonic Wars of the very early nineteenth century, cavalry could usually do little to infantry that remained in close formation, and tended to suffer badly from musketry.

By the time the American Civil War broke out in 1861, the mounted swordsman was obsolete. However, the cavalry remained the most prestigious of combat arms, drawing its traditions from the knights and gentlemen-at-arms of previous eras, and its proponents clung to the idea that well-handled cavalry could still justify their use as more than merely mounted infantry.

During the American Civil War, many cavalry units fought on foot as skirmishers, and mounted combat was often a matter for carbines, revolvers and sawn-off shotguns. Southern cavalry units tended to make more and better use of the sabre than their northern counterparts, but even they relied on their firearms as much as, or more than, their swords.

The revolver replaced the sword as a sidearm to be worn on the belt, while the sabre was carried on the saddle and only used on horseback. For the infantry officer, the sabre was best left behind as it marked him as a high-value target for enemy sharpshooters. With virtually no chance of using it in action and a high probability of attracting fire by carrying it, the sword had become a liability on the battlefield.

Yet still the sword had its advocates. Under the right conditions, could the cavalry still not employ their sabres to good effect? The answer was yes, but conditions had to be virtually perfect. During the Franco-

Prussian war of 1870, a Prussian cavalry brigade under Friedrich von Bredow was ordered to break through French infantry who were behind a line of guns – about as far from perfect conditions as was possible – in order to restore a rapidly deteriorating situation.

Von Bredow's attack made use of dead ground, i.e. a hollow that prevented the French from firing at or even detecting his cavalry as they approached. The Prussian cavalry were able to punch through the French line and exploit the opening, overrunning guns and scattering infantry. The price they paid was enormous, attracting as they did rifle fire as well as volleys from the mitrailleuse batteries nearby. These were not machine guns in the true sense, but were composed of multiple rifle barrels firing together.

Von Bredow's cavalry was then counter-attacked by French cuirassiers, bringing about a fierce cavalry melee in which the French thrust at gaps in the Prussians' body armour at the armpit or under the helmet, while the Prussians delivered cuts at any un-armoured flesh within reach. Despite heavy casualties – over 300 out of 500 men who had started the charge – the Prussian cavalry were able to retire.

This incident was in truth the last gallant hurrah of the mounted swordsman, but cavalry advocates took it as proof that there was still a role for them to play. Thus it was that in the early weeks of the Great War, the war to end all wars, French cavalry went forward to the attack wearing glittering helmets and cuirasses, looking much like they had in 1814.

Contrary to popular belief, cavalry were not immediately swept from the battlefield by machine-gun fire. It is claimed that the very first casualty inflicted by the British Army in the First World War was caused by a cavalry sabre. This weapon was a 1908 pattern light cavalry sabre (probably the 1912 officer's model), which is widely considered to be the best cavalry sword ever used by the British Army.

The 1908 sabre and its American equivalent, the 1913 'Patton' sabre, were primarily thrusting swords. Experiments conducted by the young George Patton (later a renowned armoured warfare commander) 'proved' that the point was more effective than the edge to the satisfaction of both British and American military officials. Patton's experiments involved, among other things, groups of men advancing at one another as if in a cavalry charge. He demonstrated that a thrusting sword used much like a lance would permit an effective first strike before a cut could be made, which was convincing enough to permit his design of sword to be adopted.

These last cavalry sabres could cut, of course, but they were not well suited to it. They were optimised for the thrust from horseback, and had an industrial look about them that fit well with the era. Gone were the bright uniforms and beautiful weapons of bygone eras, and the panache of the gentleman-at-arms; now the cavalry trooper was a common soldier dressed in dowdy green. He was armed with a carbine or rifle for service as mounted infantry and a utilitarian sabre for horseback combat.

On the Western Front, the early weeks of the war were characterised by mobile warfare of a traditional sort. The British and French were pushed back, pursued by German forces in a manner not dissimilar to the war of 1870. Cavalry scouted and made both attacks and counter-attacks. Prussian uhlans – lancers – clashed with French cuirassiers and British dragoons. As the war settled into stalemate and the trench deadlock began, the cavalry waited behind the lines in the hope of a breakthrough that never came.

Yet this was not the end of it. On the Eastern front, the war remained more mobile than elsewhere. Austrian, Prussian and Russian cavalry operated much like they had in the past, though the revolver and the carbine were their primary weapons now. There were occasions when cavalry brigades still met at sabre's point, far from the rifles of the infantry, and fought it out in the traditional manner.

By the end of the First World War, the sword was obviously no longer a viable weapon. For a time, cavalry continued to be issued sabres, as well as lances and rifles, but the horsed cavalry units that were fielded in the Second World War were, for the most part, mounted infantry. Meanwhile, the cavalry began its transition into a mechanised force. Sabres might be carried on parade, but they no longer had a place on the battlefield. There is no room in a tank for a sword, and hopefully little need for one.

CHAPTER 8

Alive and Well: Fencing in the Modern Era

Today, fencing is a recreational activity or a sporting contest rather than a matter of life and death. Swords are no longer carried for self-defence or as signs of personal status, and certainly they are not considered to be viable battlefield weapons. True, there are parts of the world where machetes and similar sword-like weapons are regularly used, and swords are occasionally employed by criminals or lunatics to cause mayhem, but it seems unlikely that we will see many sword-versus-sword encounters in the streets of our modern cities.

The practical aspect of swordsmanship is thus a thing of the past, at least for now. It is fascinating to speculate about what a society where guns are outlawed but swords may be worn by citizens in good standing would be like, but this is more probably the stuff of a dystopian science-fiction movie than useful speculation. Yet despite the fact that its day is long gone, the sword is still with us.

There has always been another dimension to swordsmanship, based on recreation or sporting use, or on the display of skill for its own sake. The ability to engage in highly technical salle play was an essential skill for the young gentleman who wished to impress his peers and social superiors, yet the very masters who taught these skills also admonished their pupils to eschew flashy or excessively complex technique in a serious fight. There was swordplay for the fencing salle and swordplay for the street, and they were quite different.

This social aspect to swordplay has survived long after the sword itself became outdated. The modern sport of fencing is generally associated with the higher echelons of society, and with universities. This is something of a false image – there is really no reason why anyone cannot take up the sport, and there exists a surprisingly large number of fencing clubs – but the image of an upper-class activity lingers. A similar mystique surrounds equestrian sports, even though they, too, are fairly accessible to anyone with a reasonable amount of disposable income.

The horse and the sword were once hallmarks of the social elite, and considerable effort went into keeping undesirables from the lower orders out of that elite. It is perhaps an indication of the progress that society has made that anyone, regardless of birth, can now engage in activities once barred to them. Money is an issue of course, but today's society permits ordinary people to make large fortunes from time to time.

A couple of centuries ago, someone who did so (perhaps by way of the Industrial Revolution) would be expected to adopt the manners of the upper echelons and to learn to fence if he were to be accepted. The fencing salles of 1750 or 1800 were populated largely by young men from 'new money', learning the skills necessary to be accepted by those coming from 'old money' … and suffering their scorn as they struggled to master skills that had become a social requirement, such as fencing.

Fencing was not always so well regarded, especially in England during the sixteenth and seventeenth centuries. Fencing masters were at times lumped in with vagabonds, ruffians and drunks, and were not permitted in some areas. Visiting a fencing salle has sometimes been less socially acceptable than frequenting a brothel. Something of a double standard applied here; fencing masters were ill-regarded, and visiting them was frowned upon, but skill with the sword was admired and indeed was considered the hallmark of a gentleman.

Fencing also has long traditions as a sport and as a form of entertainment. The knightly tournament and the gladiatorial spectacle before it served to entertain nobility and commoners alike, as well as honing the skills of those involved. Later, backswording was a popular entertainment as part of an event which might also include bare-knuckle fights and singlestick bouts. Challenge matches and exhibition bouts drew large crowds, especially when famous fighters were involved. These men were the sporting heroes of their day, and their technique might well have been dissected in the alehouse with the same fervour as the actions of today's athletes.

The move from both combat art and sporting activity to only the latter was a gradual one, and occurred simply because there was no longer a need for the sword to be a combat weapon. Salle play had always been a form of recreation – some masters despaired of their pupils ever taking the art seriously – and, towards the end of the nineteenth century, recreational and sport fencing became the forms in which swordsmanship would survive.

The Origins of Modern Fencing

The modern Olympic sport of fencing has its origins in small-sword play. A light training weapon with a large tip was developed to allow safe practice and recreational play. Known as a fleuret (flower) in France for the shape of the tip, it became more widely known as a foil. Duelling foils then emerged, but their use was short-lived.

Next came the épée, or épée de combat. This larger, heavier thrusting sword was developed to more closely recreate the characteristics of the duelling sword or the small-sword. Duelling épées also emerged, and the very last duels fought in France used these weapons.

The foil target was restricted to the torso, whereas the épée permitted a touch to be scored anywhere on the body. Various explanations for this have been put forward; the reality is probably a combination of factors. The nineteenth-century foil was a very light weapon, though stiffer and heavier than a modern fencing foil, so it would create a very narrow wound track. This meant that a hit anywhere but a vital organ was unlikely to stop the opponent. True, a thrust to the face or throat would seriously inconvenience anyone who received it, but it was not desirable to encourage this sort of play even after fencing masks were developed.

The wider and heavier épée was considered to be able to cause more serious injuries, and thus could score anywhere on the body. Hits to the foot may seem strange, but would discommode most people – in the small-sword era some masters advocated thrusts to the foot as a surprise move and a way to end a fight without killing the opponent. The difference in wounding characteristics also contributed to conventions; foil bouts were typically fought to five touches, whereas épéeists often fought to only one.

The restriction of the target area may also have been influenced by the style of swordsmanship training used before the fencing mask was invented. In order to prevent anyone getting 'one in the eye' (yet another figure of speech originating in the world of swordplay), the target was restricted to a plastron covering the chest.

The foil was also governed by a system of 'priority'. This assisted judging a bout and also promoted good fencing, rather than repeated jabbing of a sort all too easy to engage in with a light weapon such as a foil. Priority rules have changed somewhat over time, but the basic principle is that once a fencer establishes 'right of way' by beginning an attack, his opponent cannot score by making an attack of his own unless it is the only one that lands. In essence, this is the same as having a rule in tennis that once one player has started his serve the other cannot simply bash a ball of his own over the net and claim a point.

Exactly what constitutes an attack is a subject that has caused many an argument at the fencing club or consultation with the officials at an event. Some early conventions gave an attack with a straight arm on the lunge priority over one not on the lunge, and gave any straight-arm attack priority over one made with a jabbing action.

Later rulebooks defined an attack as a straight or straightening arm with the point threatening the opponent. Movement of the body – whether the fencer was moving forward or back, or standing still – was not relevant to this. What mattered was that his point was threatening the opponent.

Once an attack (or 'line') was established in this manner, that fencer had right of way (i.e. only his hit would score) until he either relinquished his line (e.g. by bending his arm and thus no longer threatening the target, or by taking his point off target) or it was taken away from him by a parry or similar action, such as beating his point aside. Once right of way had been taken by making a successful parry, that fencer had right of way providing he began an immediate riposte, and retained it until he relinquished it or it was taken away by a parry.

At that point, the counter-riposte had priority, and so forth until someone was hit or the phrase ended. This could occur if the fencers moved apart and began preparing to start a new phrase, or if the president (later called the referee) halted proceedings for whatever reason. This might be for safety reasons, or because an offence had been committed by one of the fencers. In training, an instructor might halt his pupils because what is sometimes referred to as a 'furball' or a 'godawful mess' had erupted and a reset seemed desirable.

This all sounds quite complex, but the principle is fairly simple. The priority system promoted good fencing and made judging easier. If, for example, a fencer attacked and was parried, and simply kept on poking at his opponent until he hit something, the parry-riposte his opponent made would score, not the repeated desperate jabs. Good fencing, with clear attacks that showed the judges and spectators that the fencer had taken a line, would prevail over jabbing with a bent arm, which in any case could be dangerous.

The priority system works well if applied properly, and it is logical. As well as promoting 'correct' fencing, it also reflects reality to some extent. A swordsman who parried an attack and made a clean riposte would inflict a far more serious injury upon his opponent than he would receive if the opponent tried to replace his point on target and push it home.

However, poor interpretation of this system could give priority to whichever fencer began charging forward first, or who shouted in jubilation the loudest after a double hit. The advent of very flexible blades and electronic scoring have made priority very difficult to interpret for experts; laypeople might have absolutely no idea what just happened.

The épée took a different approach, dispensing with priority altogether. Instead, the épée rules were based around the idea of hitting without being hit. Obviously, a hit that landed well after the first would not count (modern scoring apparatus blocks out hits arriving more than 1/20 of a second after the first) but a double hit was scored as such. This meant that a double defeat was possible, which reflects the reality of a duel quite well. Most modern competitions fence to five or more points, and continue until there is a single winner, but double-defeats are still possible in some events.

The other key difference between foil and épée play was the idea of off-target hits. A hit that landed somewhere other than the target area at foil (e.g. on the mask or the sword arm) would cause the bout to be halted and the fencers to continue from their current positions. An on-target hit caused a reset to the guard lines and a point to be scored. Any hit at épée resulted in the same, other than a hit to the floor or perhaps an unfortunate official who was standing a little too close.

Sabre Fencing

Fencing with the military sabre, and also singlestick fencing to simulate it, was primarily an armed forces exercise, although some civilian masters taught it as part of their repertoire. However, in the mid- to late nineteenth century, new kinds of sabre began to emerge. The earliest recorded gymnasium sabre in British service is from 1864, though practice sabres with a similar function were created a few years previously.

A gymnasium sabre was a practice weapon that was light enough to permit long periods of training or fencing and did not require heavy padding to prevent injury. It was heavier than the modern sporting sabre, but lighter than the military weapons then in use. Gymnasium sabres could be considered to be among the first sporting sabres, and were used in sabre *v.* sabre and sabre *v.* bayonet matches at events as grand as the 1886 and 1891 Royal Tournament.

At roughly the same time, duelling sabres were becoming popular in Italy. Chief among its exponents was Giuseppe Radaelli, who devised a light, straight-bladed sabre that was known by his name. The Radaelli sabre was not a military weapon, more closely resembling the sporting sabres we see today. This is not least because it was highly influential in their development. However, it was used in a manner highly reminiscent of the military weapon, using a moulinet to deliver the most effective cut possible with such a light blade.

Radaelli did not advocate cutting with the very tip of the weapon. This was sufficient to obtain a touch in the fencing salle or competition, but it would not cause serious enough injury to stop a determined opponent. Instead he considered that his sabre was best used to cut with the point of percussion, which lay perhaps 10–20 cm from the tip of the blade. This reduced reach, but when combined with the quite considerable body movement that Radaelli considered necessary for an effective moulinet, it would enable even a light blade to deliver a very serious injury.

Radaelli not only advocated the percussive cut for purposes of dismantling an opponent, but also felt that tip-cutting would create a false impression of the weapon's measure. Thus he did not feel that it was acceptable to use tip-cuts to obtain touches and therefore 'wins' in salle play; his system was still geared towards combat effectiveness, and eschewed any tricks that might reduce it, even if they allowed a fencer to win more bouts in the salle.

The early sabres used for sporting competition bore a strong resemblance to gymnasium- or Radaelli-type weapons, and were used in a traditional style, with moulinets and cuts made as if injury was intended. That is not to say that fencers were encouraged to lash at one another and cause pain; unnecessarily hard hitting is not good fencing. However, the sporting sabre retained its martial origins well into the mid-twentieth century.

The sabre target was defined as anything from the waist up. This was probably due to various factors, including the fact that leg cuts could be painful and required extra protection. Late nineteenth-century manuals state that leg cuts should only be permitted in a bout if suitable protection is worn. Perhaps it simply became habit to restrict the target rather than requiring fencers to struggle into and out of additional protective equipment.

It is equally or more likely that the target restriction reflected the reality of sabre combat. There was little point in slashing a horseman on the legs; he would likely be able to deliver a more telling return blow before going in search of medical assistance. It has also been suggested that the upper body was all that was reachable by a man on horseback against one on foot, though the relevance of this is debatable.

Additionally, reaching far down for a cut at the ankle left the fencer open to being hit on the head, so was not a great option for someone who hoped to survive a fight with live weapons. With practice weaponry, it became a viable method of landing a hit before his opponent could counter, essentially a trick to get a cheap point in a sporting context. It is possible that the target restriction was created to force sabre fencers to remain true to their martial heritage. Whatever the reason (or more likely, combination of reasons), the tradition has survived to this day.

The Development of Modern Fencing

Traditionally, most forms of swordsmanship used circling movements, i.e. the weapons were fenced 'in the round'. This made a lot of sense when fighting in a dark, cobbled alleyway or on the battlefield, where it was not possible to see what was behind. Likewise, most fencing systems employed a short lunge if a lunge was used at all, for reasons that were as much to do with footwear fashions as with what was underfoot.

Linear fencing became more prevalent when several pairs were training or engaging in freeplay in the salle. This helped ensure that those nearby were not endangered, nor unexpectedly involved in the bout. It also facilitated large events where multiple bouts could be ongoing at once.

A formal fencing strip, or piste, was defined as being 14 m in total length, with a centre line and guard lines each 2 m from it. Fencers started a bout behind their guard lines and returned there after a point had been scored, ensuring that they were not immediately able to hit one another upon the command to begin.

The piste was between 1.5 and 2 m wide, and had warning areas 2 m from the rear line. Leaving the piste to the side or rear with both feet scored a point for the opponent under most circumstances. Chasing an opponent over the back line was and remains a perfectly valid tactic; in that regard little has changed since the Viking Holmgang duel, in which to leave the duelling area was to be defeated and disgraced, or the early mensur, which was defined by the small circle in which the duellists fought.

Going off the piste was acceptable after moving past the opponent, which occurred on certain types of attack, but in any case the bout would be halted at the point where the fencers passed one another. Turning around to continue the fight was particularly undesirable once fencers acquired cables trailing from their backs.

Other movements were banned early on or dropped later. Voids that involved turning the back, such as the full volte, were disallowed because they exposed the unprotected back of the head. Touching one another with anything other than the weapon (known as corps à corps) was forbidden in foil and sabre, and permitted only if it occurred without violence in an épée bout. The days of smashing one another in the teeth with the pommel were well and truly over by that point.

Some voids remained part of the fencer's repertoire, though most fell out of favour. Leg slips to avoid a thrust to leg or foot, and a variety of leaning and twisting dodges, remain common. Rarely seen, but still legal, is the passata sotto. This movement is essentially a combination of a very low lunge and a ducking movement supported by the off hand. This hand is the only part of the fencer permitted to touch the floor (other than his feet!). The passata sotto is sadly not as effective as it used to be; very flexible blades can flick down into the back where in previous generations the thrust would pass over the fencer. Nevertheless, it remains an option.

The single biggest change to occur in fencing was the introduction of electric judging, which began in the 1930s for épée and the 1950s for foil. Many aspects of the modern sport came about as a result of the characteristics (or limitations) of the electric judging apparatus. Before its introduction, competitive bouts involved a president (referee) and two seconds who stood to the sides and slightly to the rear of each fencer. Their job was to raise a hand if they saw 'their' fencer land a hit on his opponent. The president would then analyse the phrase and ask the seconds if the hit was on or off target (at foil and sabre).

The problem with 'steam' fencing (as non-electric fencing perhaps inevitably became called) was that it was hard for even an attentive second to see where a fast-moving point landed, and if it hit cleanly or not. Many seconds would simply fail to see a hit at all, or might disagree. This led to many bouts going on for far too long before a clean and obvious hit was scored, though it has to be said that a fencer who made clean and clear attacks and ripostes had an advantage over a sloppy opponent or one whose style revolved around fast jabbing.

The electric apparatus was intended to determine if hits had landed, and if there was sufficient 'character of penetration' to indicate a wounding hit. This was done using a tip that was depressed to complete an electric circuit. Spring pressure ensured that a hit had to be reasonably clean and solid to register, and a circuit in the apparatus blocked out hits landing more than 1/20 of a second after the first. This might seem like a very short time, but simultaneous hits are extremely common in modern sport fencing.

The sabre, in particular, was so beset by simultaneous attacks that all manner of measures were used to try to discourage them. Crossing the feet was banned, preventing fencers running at one another or using the flèche attack. This was originally an incredible horizontal diving movement, which eventually developed into something that resembled an extremely committed attack on the pass. Simultaneous attacks remained just as common after the prohibition of this movement, however.

The problem of off-target and on-target hits was solved for the foil (it was not necessary for the épée; all hits were on target) by using an electrically conductive jacket over the on-target areas. Depressing the tip of the weapon caused a white off-target light to come on; a complete circuit made through the opponent's jacket gave a coloured on-target light, while an earthed piste made from conductive material meant that a floor hit would no longer stop the bout.

It was possible to cheat using a switch mounted on the weapon to create false hits, but this was extremely rare and relatively easy to detect in a weapons inspection. However, the electric apparatus led to changes in fencing styles. Many coaches realised that it was not necessary to fence in a pleasing or traditional manner; what mattered was triggering the electric judging apparatus.

Getting the light on did not require a clean thrust, with a slightly bent blade indicating a character of penetration. A marginal poking scrape might do it, as would a flicked hit. Some flicks, sometimes known as 'throwing the point', were fairly minor actions used to slip around a parry or get the point to the target a little quicker. However, fencers soon discovered that it was possible to make large flicking actions from the wrist or elbow, which might hit the opponent somewhere in the middle of his back.

Flicks of this sort, often delivered with a highly flexible blade developed for the purpose, were extremely hard to parry and could come in from a variety of angles. A new style of swordplay developed to use and guard against the flick-hit, which favoured the more mobile and athletic fencer. Speed and timing became the paramount attributes for success.

Sabre, too, changed direction due to electrification. A conductive jacket, mask and glove detected hits made with the blade, but unlike the foil or épée, the sabre had no wire down the blade to a button on the tip. Instead the whole blade was the conductor. This meant that the merest touch with any part of the blade on the opponent's target area triggered the lights and scored a hit. An attempt was made using accelerometers mounted on the hilt to ensure that cuts and thrusts had to be delivered in the traditional manner, but this was not a success and was soon abandoned.

Electric sabre emerged during the late 1980s – during the author's fencing and coaching career – and resulted in significant changes in technique. Sabreurs can extend their reach by attacking to touch with the very tip of the blade, or deliver a flat hit with the side of the blade. Parrying is a problem in this case, as a sporting sabre blade is very flexible in this orientation and will flick over a parry.

At one time, a hit that came over the guard in this manner was termed a 'cookie' (from coquille, the term for the guard), and was disallowed by the referee. Currently a hit is a hit, probably because modern fencing is so fast that a referee might not be able to reliably spot what is a valid hit and what is not. In fact this has become something of a problem – fencing is too fast for the average observer to really enjoy.

Various attempts have been made to make fencing more television-friendly. Rules on clothing were relaxed to make fencers more individually identifiable, and masks with a clear faceplate offered the chance to see faces previously obscured by wire mesh. The previous rather clumsy setup with fencers connected to the judging apparatus by wires running from their jackets to a spool on the ground and thence to 'the box' (the judging apparatus) was brought up to date with radio transmitters, but the fundamental problem of getting people to watch fencing remains.

The electric apparatus made judging easier in a way that made the underlying problem worse. It was hard to see whether a hit had been made, but the machine could tell. The removal of a need to be seen hitting by a human enabled fencers to move ever faster – to the point where people who would enjoy watching a sword fight cannot make head or tail of what is going on. The situation is fine for the competitors themselves, but to an outside audience it is less attractive.

The solution, perhaps, might be a retrograde step. The electric apparatus, when introduced, had limitations that do not exist today. An addition to the circuit that required the tip to remain depressed for a short interval would force a return to direct thrusts rather than flicks. This would make the match more enjoyable to watch, as it would require a return to more traditional technique.

The use of heavier, stiffer blades that could not flick would also force the return of traditional swordplay, which would surely attract more spectators. This would require a change in equipment, but that is nothing new. During the author's own career, standards changed repeatedly, with the clothing requirement moving from a simple thick cotton jacket to increasingly protective grades of Kevlar with an under-plastron protecting the armpit area. Today's fencers are all but bulletproof.

The current problem facing the fencing world is that the sport has evolved into something that the general public does not enjoy watching, but the competitors and their coaches seem happy with. A move to something that looks more like traditional swordplay would require major changes in technique and training methods, and since so much effort has been committed to producing fencers tailored to the current system, a change is highly unlikely.

Historical Fencing

There are in fact two activities that call themselves 'fencing'. Both involve swordplay, but they take very different approaches. Where Olympic-style or 'sport' fencing has evolved into something with its own identity, the other form of fencing – historical fencing – seeks to retain the traditional character of what are collectively known as the Historical European Martial Arts (HEMA).

HEMA is, as the name suggests, concerned with the martial (i.e. fighting) aspects of swordplay, rather than the current competition rules. Some HEMA students treat what they do as what amounts to experimental archaeology, seeking to understand what it was to fight with the swords of previous generations. Others are more interested in the practical aspects, and are fencers rather than historians. Most fall somewhere in between.

HEMA is a modern term, but historical fencing has its origins in the late nineteenth century, when Captain Alfred Hutton, along with his friends, including Sir Richard Burton and Edgerton Castle, pioneered a revival of interest in 'old sword play'. In addition to putting forward a system for military sabre that he hoped would be adopted by the British Army (and a sword designed for use with it), Hutton fostered interest in the rapier and other ancient sword systems.

Hutton's work was interrupted by the First World War, in which many students of historical fencing perished. He did, however, make a lasting contribution to the world of fencing in the form of manuals that reiterated some of the ancient masters' work, and helped set up the Amateur Fencing Association. This organisation survives to this day as British Fencing, the governing body for sport fencing in the United Kingdom.

Historical fencing did not quite perish, but did not become popular until quite recently. Re-enactment groups 'live' the history of various periods, and include Romans, Celts, Vikings and medieval knights. Not all re-enactment groups fight with weapons of course, but knightly tournaments and clashes of 'barbarian' warriors make a colourful spectacle that draws large crowds to historic sites. Re-enactment groups also do good work in researching their period of interest, and have created a wealth of historical discovery by trying to live like people of their chosen era.

Organisations like the Society for Creative Anachronism aim to keep alive the crafts, skills and the general 'feeling' of the Middle Ages and the Renaissance. Organised into 'kingdoms' and well regulated with rules for heraldry and social advancement, as well as armed combat, the SCA has over 30,000 members, and engages in large events, which include hand weapons and archery tournaments.

Armoured combat and rapier duelling are an important part of SCA events, and are regulated to make combat as realistic as possible without being unsafe. Fights are not for points; the intent is to deliver strokes that would, in the view of the judges, kill or incapacitate the opponent. As might be expected, training is offered in how to use weapons effectively but also safely.

Most historical fencing groups follow similar concepts in their weapons use, but tend to be more about modern people studying historical swordsmanship than any attempt to recreate the past. Technique is authentic as far as possible, and weapons are designed to replicate their historical equivalents, but the general feeling of a historical fencing group tends to be more like a martial arts class or (sport) fencing club than a re-enactment society.

The historical fencing community is growing, and is to a great extent subdivided into groups studying medieval weapons and those more interested in later eras. There is a lot of crossover; many large events have participants from all segments of the historical fencing community. However, a great many groups specialise in one particular aspect of the field.

The historical fencing community hosts a number of tournaments, which can be considered to fall into the categories of 'fencing' and 'fighting' events. Fencing events are typically held with weapons such as the rapier, small-sword and sabre, and have rules prohibiting grappling and general rough-housing. Longsword, backsword and similar events are typically 'fighting' tournaments and can be rather more intense.

With so many historical styles to study, most groups specialise in one or more areas. Thus a tournament might pit a rapier fencer who has trained in the Italian style of Capoferro against one favouring the Spanish system of Thibault, or an English-style sabreur against a Polish opponent. Outside the tournament environment it can be interesting to see how a nineteenth-century military sabre fares against a fifteenth-century sidesword. This sort of informal experimentation can help historians or interested laymen understand how and why fencing systems evolved in the way that they did.

It is one thing to see a stroke or parry illustrated in an ancient fencing manual, and quite another to feel the blade shiver as it makes contact with the parry. Practical experimentation or running through plays from an ancient text imparts a level of understanding that cannot be found in words and pictures.

Likewise, a weapon in a museum is just a thing to be admired. It is a quite different experience to hold a sword, to feel how it moves and how the body mechanics of the swordsman change the behaviour of the blade. Some weapons seem to leap towards the opponent on a cut, or align themselves effortlessly for the thrust. Others seem strangely clumsy until an expert demonstrates how to make them come alive. It is only by this sort of hands-on experience that we can begin to understand what it was to use these weapons in a life-or-death situation.

The Enduring Mystique of the Sword

The sword was never as historically decisive as many other weapons. Spears and axes had a greater impact on the conduct of warfare and the outcomes of it, and of course the invention of reliable firearms changed the whole nature of combat. Yet the sword remains an enduring symbol of strength, nobility, justice and other concepts that are generally considered to be positive.

The sword is a concept more than it is a specific weapon. In the Old Testament, the leader of the Hebrews, Joshua, kills the king of Hazor 'with a sword'. This would be a very different weapon from the cruciform arming sword of the medieval nobleman or the sabre of a Napoleonic cavalry trooper. It would have been a sickle-sword, a weapon of almost axe-like design, but it was a sword in name and in spirit.

Throughout history, the sword is a constant. Its shape and design vary and the techniques for its use evolve constantly, but it is always there as a symbol as well as a fighting tool. Military officers of the Age of Reason and the Napoleonic Era did not really expect to use their swords in battle, but they were carried as a badge of rank. Today, swords are still worn by military personnel and some officials on ceremonial occasions.

The formal dress for a Finnish PhD recipient includes a small-sword. It is hard to see a connection between academic excellence and the need to carry a weapon; it is likely that there is none. Instead, the sword is symbolic of high status, prestige and perhaps trust. Swords have traditionally been presented as weapons of honour – few other weapon types are considered appropriate, although there are exceptions.

Similarly, swordsmanship has always been considered the hallmark of a gentleman, and retains some of this mystique. Many people react differently to hearing that an individual is a fencer than they would to a player of other sports. Responses are typically surprised, and range from contempt for such highbrow nonsense to questions about whether the swords are really sharp or if it is possible to see out of the mask. There is usually some waving around of an arm in a vaguely swordish manner, and a question about whether it's like whatever recent movie has featured swordplay.

Fencing is as mundane as any other sport or activity. It requires a certain amount of effort to learn but is in no way beyond the capabilities of the average person. Yet so much of the mystique of the sword remains that fencing is somehow considered to be different to many other activities.

Perhaps this lingering perception is connected with the people who are seen with swords today. Royalty, senior officials and military personnel wear swords; ordinary people do not. Perhaps it has more to do with the images portrayed by games, books, movies and television. Hollywood would like us to believe that the Japanese katana is the ultimate weapon, but the pantheon of European swords has its place in fiction too.

Swords, it seems, are the weapons of heroes. A skilled swordsman, we are led to believe, can escape unscathed from a horde of musket-armed soldiers or deal with numerous assailants of a lesser sort. The only real opposition for a swordsman is another swordsman, who will usually require some acrobatics, witty banter and unlikely feats of bladesmanship to defeat. This is entertaining nonsense, but it does reflect the status of the sword in Western society. It is not the cause of the mystique of the sword but an effect of it.

Centuries of swordsmanship have created figures of speech that many of their users do not realise are sword-related. A point well made in argument is greeted with the acknowledgement 'touché' – usually pronounced 'toosh' and meaning 'touch' in the sense of a point scored in a fencing match. An aggressive posture in international politics is 'sabre-rattling', and a person displaying excessive bravado might be said to be 'trailing his sabre'.

The latter comes from a habit, particularly among French light cavalrymen, of trailing the metal chape of their sabre scabbard along the ground, making a noise to announce their presence. Anyone protesting would be doing so in the face of an armed man who was, quite likely, looking for a fight. The sword in this case was both the means of picking a fight and the method of deterring or winning it; it was the symbol and the tool of a man who thought himself above others and was willing to fight or even kill (and thus also to risk his life) to prove it.

This, perhaps, is the essence of the sword. It is nothing more than a well-crafted piece of metal that may be functional or beautiful, or both, but it is nothing if it is simply left hanging on a wall or standing in a corner. The sword only becomes important when it is used for something

– to settle a matter of honour, to fight in battle or self-defence, or to point the way forward for a regiment.

The mystique of the sword, then, comes not from its form or even its possible function, but from the manner in which it was used and by whom. Although not the most effective of all weapons, the sword was easy to carry yet capable of heroic individual combat. It was subtle enough to display beautiful technique, and lethal enough to dispose of any enemy. It was also a thing of beauty, adorning the gentleman or the officer as well as deterring his enemies and reminding his subordinates that he held power over them.

The sword did not shape European history. It did not carve out empires or build civilisations. It did not lead armies to victory or discover new lands across the oceans. But these things were done by men for whom the sword was both tool and symbol, creating an association that endures to this day. Enshrined within our culture the idea lives on that a great man requires a sword, and that a man with a sword can achieve almost anything.